JULIEN BITOUN

GUITARS & HEROES

MYTHIC GUITARS AND LEGENDARY MUSICIANS

FIREFLY BOOKS

A FIREFLY BOOK

Published by Firefly Books Ltd. 2018

First printing

Publisher Cataloging-in-Publication Data (U.S.)

Library of Congress Control Number: 2018935495

Library and Archives Canada Cataloguing in Publication

Bitoun, Julien
[Guitars & heroes. English]
     Guitars and heroes : mythical guitars and legendary musicians / Julien Bitoun.
Published originally in French under title: Guitars & heroes : guitares mythiques et musiciens de légende.
Includes index.
ISBN 978-0-228-10118-5 (softcover)
     1. Guitar--History. 2. Guitarists. I. Title. II. Title: Guitars & heroes. English
ML1015.G9B62413 2018   787.8709   C2018-901306-0

Published in the United States by
Firefly Books (U.S.) Inc.
P.O. Box 1338, Ellicott Station
Buffalo, New York 14205

Published in Canada by
Firefly Books Ltd.
50 Staples Avenue, Unit 1
Richmond Hill, Ontario L4B 0A7

ACKNOWLEDGMENTS

To Anna, without whom I never would have found the inclination to get up at the crack of dawn and write this volume.

To Philippe, without whom I never would have met Luc-Edouard.

To Luc-Edouard, without whom I never would have met Philippe.

To Carole, Émilie, Nicolas, and Philippe, the team of shock-troopers without whom this little book would have remained nothing more than a set of Open Office files totally lacking in panache.

To Mike Eldred, John Page, and JW Black, who put me on the right path when it came to tracking down Don Was' bass.

To the turquoise Strat Custom Shop 69 that I played between two chapters.

To the artists whose music I listened to while writing this book: Badfinger, At the Drive-In, John Zorn, Laura Cox, Ornette Coleman, Jack White, Muddy Waters, St. Vincent, The Collectors, Gorillaz, Greg Kihn, Body Count, and, as always, AC/DC and the Beatles.

JULIEN BITOUN

Created by olo.éditions
www.oloeditions.com
115, rue d'Aboukir
75002 Paris, France

SIX STRINGS, TEN FINGERS

Few musical instruments are as personal as a guitar. Professional pianists generally have to perform on whichever piano happens to be in place at the concert venue, while drummers often have to adapt to the kit that is put at their disposal. For a guitarist, this kind of approach is unthinkable, so close is the bond between the piece of wood and the music.

Even so, every guitarist builds an intimate relationship with the six strings in his or her own unique way, and when we chart the wide variety of these relationships, we end up with an unexpected and exhilarating map. From avid collectors to those bound by ties of passion to a single love, via the inveterate DIY brigade, each guitar-guitarist couple has its own distinct way of working, which often reveals a hidden aspect of the performer's artistic approach. Here, therefore, is a series of portraits at the meeting point of six strings and ten fingers.

THE ART IN ITS INFANCY

DELTA BLUES AND ROCKABILLY

08

The guitar, as it is played today, traces its origins right back to the Mississippi delta, in the early days of the 20th century. The pioneers of rural blues established multiple musical customs that are second nature to us today, and the very first rock 'n' roll virtuosos from the 1950s, the age of rockabilly, served as a conduit for this culture.

THE GOLDEN AGE

SURF, GARAGE ROCK, PSYCHEDELIA

86

The Americans, in turn, rediscovered their own music through the prism of the British bands, and threw themselves into some wonderful experiments with sound. The watchword was simple: DIY, or "Do It Yourself." Enlightened amateurs thus threw themselves into rock with whatever resources were at hand, and with an unprecedented enthusiasm.

THE MODERN AGE

GRUNGE AND ALTERNATIVE ROCK

172

The guitar finally got its revenge in the early 1990s, when grunge and alternative or independent rock reminded the world that the fad for synthesized music and the rhythm box had had its day, and that it was time to go back to more basic and effective values. This was in some ways a second punk and garage revolution.

THE ART IN ITS INFANCY

DELTA BLUES AND ROCKABILLY

08

CHICAGO BLUES AND JAZZ

36

BRITISH BLUES BOOM

60

GIBSON L-1 ROBERT JOHNSON

A CHEAP INSTRUMENT

One of just two photos ▶ of Robert Johnson known to exist, in which he holds a Kalamazoo KG-14.

THE BLUESMAN ROBERT JOHNSON REPRESENTS ONE OF THE GREAT FOUNDING MYTHS OF BLUES and rock 'n' roll. This gangly character, of whom only two photos are known to exist along with some forty tracks etched onto acetate, unleashed more passions and fantasies than any other artist since. We know that he died in 1938, aged just 27; we also know that he could play and sing like nobody else, and that he influenced all the musicians of the 1960s, who made ample use of his legacy. A pact with the devil accounts both for his supernatural talent and for his early death. The same sense of mystery surrounds Johnson's guitars, and the experts have pondered long and hard over the scraps of information available to us. Like most bluesmen from the southern United States in his era, he was a hobo, an itinerant musician who moved from town to town and from woman to woman, scraping a living through his music. In light of this, it seems unlikely that he would have been a one-guitar man, and on closer inspection, the two known photos of him have a lot to say on this subject. In the most famous photo, the one in which Johnson is wearing a hat, the guitar he's playing can be seen very clearly: it is a Gibson L-1, a bottom-of-the-line model that would have already been a little out of date, since the manufacturers have identified it as dating from 1926, around a decade before the photo was taken. This was the guitar that Gibson took as its starting point when it created the posthumous signature model.

The other photo, though, in which Johnson is seen smoking a cigarette, tells a different story. Even though we can only see the neck and a small section of the body, it is nonetheless possible to identify the instrument as a Kalamazoo KG-14. Kalamazoo, named after the town in Michigan where its factory was located, was the name for two lines of guitars that were in fact made by Gibson. These instruments produced by the famous brand offered a low-spec finish; as such, they were intended for less affluent musicians who had been through the Great Depression, while not compromising the name of Gibson itself. We will never know whether the two guitars belonged to him or whether they had been lent to him for the photo, and we will never know whether they are indeed the same guitars that can be heard in his recordings. It's a mystery that will live on forever — and maybe it's better that way.

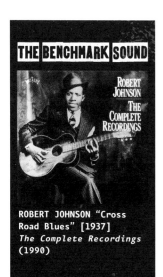

THE BENCHMARK SOUND

ROBERT JOHNSON "Cross Road Blues" [1937]
The Complete Recordings (1990)

◀ The Gibson Robert Johnson was released in the 1990s, sixty years after the bluesman's death.

STELLA
LEADBELLY
BIG VOICE, BIG GUITAR

With the trumpeter ▶
Bunk Johnson
in New York in 1946.

HUDDIE LEDBETTER, BETTER KNOWN BY HIS NICKNAME LEADBELLY, WAS A MODERN TROUBADOUR FROM THE SOUTHERN UNITED STATES AT THE TURN OF THE 19TH CENTURY. This giant figure knew so many traditional songs that the music historians Alan and John Lomax managed to secure his release from prison so that they could record him, and it was his versions of these songs that were later covered by artists as diverse as Bob Dylan, Creedence Clearwater Revival, and Nirvana. Everything about him was larger than life: his enormous and authoritative voice; his hands, the size of paddles; and the quick-to-erupt rage that earned him several spells behind bars. He therefore needed a guitar that was every bit as gigantic as he was, and so, though he sometimes played the accordion, his main instrument was a twelve-string Stella. Stella was a brand that specialized in entry-level instruments, guitars that even a poor musician could afford. The model chosen by Leadbelly was special in a number of ways. Firstly, it was a twelve-string guitar, with the usual six strings doubled, resulting in a richer, more powerful and resonant sound. On top of that, the guitar was designed to be tuned two tones lower than normal, to *C* rather than *E*, hence the cavernous depth of Leadbelly's notes. Finally, the guitar was the largest in the manufacturer's catalogue, even though it looked like a little toy in the hands of its owner. Given that he sang on his own, this richness of sound enabled him to accompany

his voice without the guitar's seeming muted, and even to develop the instrumental parts without the lack of a rhythm section making itself felt. Before performing his cover of "Where Did You Sleep Last Night?" Kurt Cobain used to tell, on stage, the story of how he had been offered the chance to buy Leadbelly's guitar, but had considered the asking price too high. That said, the guitar used for the acoustic tracks on the album *Nevermind* is indeed a Stella.

◀ *Stella Leadbelly in 1937, the year in which* Life *magazine published its famous article about him.*

MARTIN 000-45
JIMMIE RODGERS
THE GUITAR THAT SAYS THANK YOU

▲
One of the promotional photos for the singing brakeman.

WHENEVER A NEW MOVEMENT EMERGES IN MUSIC, IT IS ALMOST ALWAYS THE RESULT OF A COLLECTIVE SURGE OF CREATIVITY, WHICH MANIFESTS ITSELF THROUGH THE WORK OF SEVERAL DIFFERENT ARTISTS AT THE SAME TIME. In the case of country music, the birth of this genre whose importance in the US is difficult to overstate can be attributed to a single singer, who created a revolution all of his own: Jimmie Rodgers, dubbed "the singing brakeman." He worked on the railroads while simultaneously trying to further his career as a musician, until he was forced by a bout of tuberculosis, which took his life at the age of 35 in 1933, to dedicate himself entirely to music.

His first recordings, made in 1927, marked a turning point in the history of music, both through their enormous popular success, which instantly created a new trend, and through the considerable influence they had on later generations, with singers like Elvis Presley and Bob Dylan being among Jimmie Rodgers' fans. A key track in establishing Rodgers' formula was "Blue Yodel," a blend of blues, folk, and yodeling, the singing technique originating in the Swiss mountains of the Tyrol. For these early recordings, he accompanied himself on a brand new Martin 00-18, a guitar that was both plain (with hardly any decoration) and unpretentious (the body is made of mahogany, a very affordable wood).

Following his success, he placed an order later that year for a special model made by Martin, a 000-45. The 45 series was the manufacturer's top-of-the-line guitar in any case, but Rodgers made his even more special by asking to have his name inlaid on the fingerboard. The final detail can be found on the back of the guitar, where we find the word "Thanks" written in big yellow letters. The thinking behind this? While standing on stage between songs, Jimmie would turn the guitar around, and it would thus be the instrument that expressed his gratitude to the adoring crowds. After his death, Rodgers' widow lent the 000-45 to the singer Ernest Tubb. The Texas Troubadour would go on to use the guitar for forty years.

When Martin re-released the guitar in 1997, they felt that owing to the fact that it had had two such prominent owners, it was one of the most important guitars in the history of the United States. Leaving all exaggeration aside, it is without doubt the guitar that would have the best stories to tell.

◄ Jimmie Rodgers'
famous Martin
000-45 and the
message on its back.

MARTIN D-45
GENE AUTRY
THE SINGING COWBOY PLAYS TO THE GALLERY

▲ The western Oh, Susanna! (1936) takes its title from the traditional song that features in it several times.

IT'S HARD NOWADAYS TO PICTURE THE ALL-AMERICAN COWBOY WITHOUT A GUITAR IN HIS HANDS. EVERY BIT AS INDISPENSABLE AS HIS STETSON OR HIS HORSE, THE INSTRUMENT BECAME INSEPARABLE FROM THE MAN in the popular imagination during the age of the westerns of the 1930s. In this period, at the height of the Great Depression, the public sought myths that would allow them to change the way they thought, and the bold and fearless cowboy was certainly able to do that. Not content with being hotshot marksmen, most of them were also accomplished singers and guitarists who released records whenever they were not acting in films, of which a huge number were churned out at an industrial rate.

The most famous singing cowboy of all was, of course, Gene Autry, the ultimate hero, whose horse, Trigger, even became a star in his own right. The riders of the great plains could never be accused of restraint, either in the costumes they wore or in the guitars they played. Autry's instruments were every bit as colorful as the kitsch wonders played by the stars of country over the subsequent decades. Like his idol, Jimmie Rodgers, he wanted a top-of-the-line Martin, so he too placed an order for a series 45 with his name inlaid in mother-of-pearl on the fingerboard. But whereas Rodgers had opted for the style classed as 000, Autry had chosen the enormous dreadnought model, the biggest guitar ever made by Martin. He can lay claim

to having been given the first ever D-45 in history in 1933, and one of the first three D-45s with twelve frets clear of the body to be made in the pre-war period. He then took possession of two Gibson J-200s, the biggest model produced by Kalamazoo, in 1938; they were both also embellished with extravagant decorative elements, but these models were to remain unique items, never intended for the mass market. The general public would instead have to make do with little cowboy guitars decorated with scenes from westerns painted on the top, low-level instruments made by the firm Harmony, operating out of Chicago, and sold under the brand names Melody, Roundup, or Supertone in department stores or via mail order catalogs. It wasn't until 1994 that the luckiest fans were able to get their hands on one of a limited edition of 66 Martin D-45 guitars, modelled on Gene Autry's guitar.

◄ The white Stetson goes wonderfully well with the D-45: it's as if they were made for one another.

5 FiLMS IN WHICH GUITARS HAVE PRiDE OF PLACE

WHEN ROCK 'N' ROLL FIRST ARRIVED ON THE SCENE, THE RECORD COMPANIES SOON REALIZED THAT CINEMA WAS A GREAT WAY OF GETTING THEIR YOUNG TALENTS SOME EXPOSURE WITHOUT HAVING TO SEND THEM ALL OVER THE WORLD. AND WHAT ABOUT IN REAL FILMS, ONES THAT WEREN'T DESIGNED SOLELY AS PROMOTIONAL TOOLS? YOU'LL OFTEN FIND GUITARS POPPING UP IN THEM TOO, AND THAT'S THE CASE IN THESE FIVE MUST-SEE FEATURE FILMS.

CROSSROADS (1986), BY WALTER HiLL ▶

Crossroads *(not to be confused with the film of the same name starring Britney Spears!) managed to revive the myth of Robert Johnson in the popular imagination in the 1980s, unleashing a huge resurgence of interest in the great bluesman. The film, which tells the story of a young guitarist learning his trade in the blues from an old harmonica player, benefits from having Ry Cooder as its musical director and contains a legendary guitar duel between the protagonist and the devil's guitarist, played by Steve Vai himself.*

THE EDGE   JIMMY PAGE   JACK WHITE

IT MiGHT GET LOUD (2008), BY DAViS GUGGENHEIM ▶

A documentary with magnificent production values, presenting the world of three guitarists with very different approaches: Jack White, Jimmy Page, and The Edge. We learn about their material, their approach, and their influences, before the film culminates with the three men coming together to discuss their plans, in an upbeat atmosphere that makes for irresistible viewing.

"THE FUNNIEST ROCK MOVIE EVER MADE."

Merrill Shindler—Los Angeles Magazine

"HILARIOUS...SENDS UP WHAT THE BEATLES STARTED WITH 'A HARD DAYS NIGHT.'"

Bruce Williamson—Playboy

"DON'T MISS IT...ONE OF THE FUNNIEST MOVIES"

Stephen Shaefer—US Magazine

◄ THIS IS SPINAL TAP (1984), BY ROB REINER

It would be unthinkable to leave out this famous "mockumentary" referenced so often and in so many ways by musicians and fans of music, such is the extent to which its most celebrated lines — "this one goes up to 11" or "Hello Cleveland" — apply perfectly to the day-to-day life of a rock band. The cast are fantastic, the music is superb, and the scene in which we are introduced to the guitar collection compiled by Nigel Tufnel, the band's lead singer, makes the film worth re-watching over and over again.

SWEET AND LOWDOWN (1999), BY WOODY ALLEN ►

In this movie imagining the life of Emmet Ray, the gypsy jazz guitarist is a keen fan of Django, whom he meets at the end of a particularly moving scene. The film shows how the price of his enormous talent was a disjointed and uprooted way of life, set to the beat of a soundtrack that is an undisguised tribute to the greatest gypsy of them all.

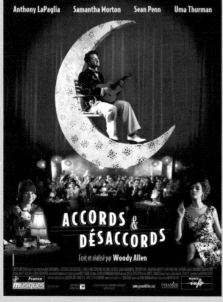

▲ TENACIOUS D IN THE PICK OF DESTINY (2006), BY LIAM LYNCH

This comedy may not have caused a sensation among film critics, but that doesn't mean it's not a very fine tribute to the passion musicians feel for their instrument. The plot revolves around the rock duo Tenacious D, providing a pretext for some excellent songs played on superb guitars (not least a black acoustic Gibson). Dave Grohl plays the role of Satan, with Ben Stiller cast as a shop assistant at Guitar Center...what more could you want?

GIBSON SOUTHERN JUMBO WOODY GUTHRIE
THE FASCIST-KILLING MACHINE

WOODY GUTHRIE WAS A FOLK SINGER WITH UNRIVALED POPULARITY IN THE ERA OF THE DUST BOWL AND THE GREAT DEPRESSION, OF ALL THE PICKET LINES AND THE SOCIAL conflicts of a particularly difficult period in United States history. His songwriting style was simple and effective, to such an extent that a song like "This Land Is Your Land" became a kind of unofficial national anthem, sung by Bruce Springsteen and Pete Seeger in 2009 at Barack Obama's inauguration ceremony. Woody Guthrie was also the archetypal folk singer/songwriter, and served as a father figure for Bob Dylan, who is always effusive in his praise of Guthrie. One of the first songs Dylan ever recorded, moreover, was "Song To Woody."

As one might expect of someone with his political convictions, Guthrie was no materialist, so was never particularly attached to his guitars. He therefore worked his way through several acoustic guitars, the only common feature of which was that they were the most rustic models with the smallest amount of decoration. At various times he was known to play a Slingerland May Bell (a low-spec product perfect for taking on the road), a classic guitar with nylon strings, a Martin 000-18 (a special tribute model was released in 2000), an 0-17 and an 0-15 (two models with small bodies made entirely of mahogany, the cheapest models produced by Martin).

The two guitars that are the most emblematic of all when it comes to Guthrie, however, have that status precisely because of their decoration. In 1941, when Nazism was

prospering in Europe, the guitarist had his picture taken holding a Gibson LG-00 adorned with the slogan "This Machine Kills Fascists." The same slogan can be found on a Gibson Southern Jumbo, which served as the basis for a special Gibson that paid tribute to Guthrie, and is seen in the best-known photos of him. This notion of the guitar as a machine for killing fascists was to become a very important inspiration for all the politically engaged folk singers of the 1960s, starting with Pete Seeger, and it can be found on guitars played by artists as varied as Donovan and KT Tunstall.

In France, it inspired a beautiful piece of writing by Jacques Higelin, entitled: "Est-ce que ma guitare est un fusil?" ("Is my guitar a gun?")

The Gibson Woody Guthrie SJ recreates the design of the Southern Jumbo from 1945.
▼

This little Gibson LG-00 ▶
is the first to feature
the famous slogan.

MARTIN D-28
HANK WILLIAMS

THE WORKHORSE

FAR FROM THE SPANGLES AND FURBELOWS OF NASHVILLE COUNTRY, THE ALABAMA NATIVE HANK WILLIAMS WAS BUSY IMPOSING HIS SOBER, DRY, AND RISKY STYLE ON HIS UNBELIEVABLE TALENT FOR WRITING.

Today, his classic hits from the 1940s still sound undeniably fresh: his melodies are clear, his brilliant lyrics earned him the nickname "the hillbilly Shakespeare," and his guitar-playing holds everything together with assurance and restraint.

The dreadnought, a huge, purring Martin guitar with a solid sound devoid of malice, was the natural workhorse for Hank. His choice fell on the very sober D-28, a very high-quality guitar with minimal decoration, unfazed by the relentless blows of its owner's pick.

Williams died in 1953 at the age of 29, leaving behind two D-28s covered with scars. A model from 1941 was owned for a while by Bob Dylan before ending up in Neil Young's guitar case. Young still plays it today all over the world, while a model from 1944 was used by his son Hank Williams Jr. and is now on display at the Country Music Hall of Fame in Nashville. It's easy to imagine which of the two guitars is having the more fun.

The Martin D-28 in its current standard form, a classic that has reigned supreme since the 1930s.
▼

HANK WILLIAMS   exclusively on   M-G-M Records

▲
Hank Williams poses with his Martin for a promotional photo.

MARTIN D-35
JOHNNY CASH
THE GUITAR IN BLACK

JOHNNY CASH WILL BE FOREVER REMEMBERED AS COUNTRY MUSIC'S "MAN IN BLACK," THE OUTLAW WHO CHERISHED HIS SOMBER OUTFITS AS A SIGN OF SOLIDARITY WITH THE OPPRESSED of this world. Though he started out with a customized Gibson J-200 and a traditional Martin dreadnought, two large guitars that went well with his intimidating stature, it's no surprise that his instrument ultimately came to reflect his sartorial style. He therefore contacted Martin to request a black dreadnought, but the company's senior management refused to countenance the idea, taking the view that a Martin guitar must always be a Martin guitar: instantly recognizable and free from all extraneous decoration. Staff at the company then decided to find a way of getting round the directives, and they had a black D-35 built for Cash. The cat finally got out of the bag in the most unlikely possible way: via the episode of *Columbo* from 1974 in which Johnny Cash plays the role of Tommy Brown, a gospel singer who has murdered his wife. Cash can be seen singing a little ballad in the episode — strumming on the illicitly made guitar as he does so.

By an irony of fate, Johnny Cash's signature black D-35 was re-released in 1996 and is now one of the brand's biggest sellers.

▲
An American legend meets two others: Columbo, Johnny Cash, and Martin.

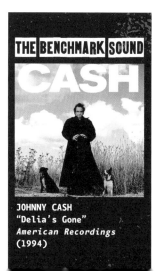

THE BENCHMARK SOUND

JOHNNY CASH
"Delia's Gone"
American Recordings
(1994)

TRIGGER
WILLIE NELSON
AS LONG AS IT LASTS

Willie Nelson on stage ▶ in 2013, accompanied by his son Micah on drums.

IN 1969, WILLIE NELSON WAS ALREADY A SEASONED SONGWRITER, WHOSE SONGS HAD BECOME HITS FOR SOME OF THE GREATEST ARTISTS IN NASHVILLE. He was tired of living in the shadows, however, and was trying to make a name for himself as a singer. One evening, an audience member got a little too carried away and ended up crushing his Guild guitar, leaving him with no option but to replace it. It was then that he came across a Martin N-20 in a musical instrument shop. This unusual model had just been released, and was an attempt on the part of the makers of the Nazareth to please classical guitarists. But its combination of nylon strings, a short scale (for a classical guitar). and a soundboard made of spruce (a wood typically used by folk musicians, whereas classical guitars are generally made with cedar soundboards) was not to many people's liking at the time. Willie Nelson, though, saw it as a good way of getting close to the sound created by Django Reinhardt, who had always been his idol, hence this very surprising choice.

A few months later, this guitar survived a fire that broke out at the singer's house, and he took it with him when he moved to Austin, Texas, where he developed a unique artistic style. His drawling voice was at the heart of this style, of course, but the taut sound of the new guitar had a role to play as well. He attained a unique sound by playing it with a pick and electrifying it with the help of a sensor, which he plugged into enormous amplifiers. This very unusual formula worked wonders, and he christened his guitar Trigger, a reference to the much-loved horse of the singing cowboy, Roy Rogers. Just like the horse that shared its name, Trigger the guitar was a trusty companion that Nelson could always rely on, and it is now impossible to imagine one of them without the other.

The years went by, and Trigger began to show the tell-tale signs of its age just as Willie Nelson did, a kind of *Picture of Dorian Gray* that wouldn't protect its subject. The pianist Leon Russell was the first of a very long line of musicians who signed the soundboard, before the blows from the pick ended up making a big hole in the guitar's body. Replacing it with a guitar in better condition was out of the question for Nelson, however. Martin released a Trigger tribute model, recreating it exactly as it was on the day it was bought, so that it was up to the new owner to give it some fresh battle-scars.

THE BENCHMARK SOUND

WILLIE NELSON
"Time Of the Preacher"
Red Headed Stranger
(1975)

"IT WAS A GOOD DAY WHEN I GOT HiM."

◀ Few guitars are as instantly recognizable as Trigger.

The Martin ▶
D-28M features
the same leather
trim as King's
original D-28.

THE BENCHMARK SOUND

ELVIS PRESLEY "That's
All Right (Mama)"
The Sun Sessions (1954)

MARTIN D-28
ELVIS PRESLEY
THE TOOL FOR A REVOLUTION

Elvis Presley received ▶
his star on the Hollywood
Walk of Fame in 1996.

ON JULY 5, 1954, AN OBSCURE CLERK NAMED ELVIS AARON PRESLEY WALKED INTO SUN STUDIO IN MEMPHIS, WHERE THE STUDIO OWNER, SAM PHILLIPS, HAD SET ASIDE SOME TIME FOR HIM TO RECORD A FEW SONGS accompanied by his two in-house musicians, Scotty Moore on guitar and Bill Black on bass. In an interval between takes, the young Elvis started singing his own take on a rural blues song that wasn't on the program, the two others joined in, and Phillips had the presence of mind to record this magical moment. The resulting song, "That's All Right (Mama)," became Elvis Presley's first single, a song that is often described as representing the birth of rock 'n' roll.

Three months after these sessions, the man later known as the King was starting to make a name for himself, and he got his hands on a serious guitar for the concerts that were to follow: a Martin 000-18. One month later, he realized that he preferred the big sound of a dreadnought and so swapped it for a D-18, and, just as it did with all its other customers, the store gave him some stickers so that he could write his name on his guitar case. Elvis, always on the lookout for an arresting stage accessory, stuck them to the soundboard of his guitar, and his pick strokes were so strong that the "S" eventually fell off, hence the nickname given to this guitar: the "Elvi."

Less than a year later, he went back to the same shop and opted for the same type, with

an upgrade in the kind of wood used: he went from having a D-18 with a mahogany body to a D-28 made of rosewood. At the same time, he picked up a leather cover intended to decorate his guitar by surrounding it with floral patterns, in the middle of which the singer's name can be seen, in capital letters. This was to be the guitar through which the revolution took place, for 1955 was the year in which Elvis made waves around the world. He released his first album with RCA early in 1956 and the image on the album sleeve, copied and parodied a thousand times (notably by The Clash for *London Calling*), shows him on stage with the D-28. The most observant will note, moreover, that his *A* string wasn't able to withstand his vigorous attack.

THE ART IN ITS INFANCY

STRATOCASTER

SUNBURST AND LEATHER

Buddy Holly (right) with ▶
Waylon Jennings in 1959
in the photo booth at New
York's Grand Central Station.

ELVIS MAY HAVE BEEN THE KING OF
FLEDGLING ROCK 'N' ROLL, BUT THE
COOLEST ROCKER IN THE SECOND HALF
OF THE 1950S WAS, WITHOUT QUESTION,
THIS YOUNG TEXAN, WHO HELPED BRING
ABOUT THE FIRST PART OF THE KING'S
STORY IN 1955. Buddy Holly didn't have
Presley's obvious good looks, but the look
with which he will forever be associated, that
of the class *nerd*, complete with suit and
thick-framed glasses, had a liberating effect
for the likes of John Lennon and later Elvis
Costello or Rivers Cuomo (Weezer). Had he
been merely a singer, this look might well
have gone unnoticed; when it was juxtaposed
with his guitar, however, the result was quite
brilliant, creating an undeniably cool
appearance. Buddy played a guitar that was
largely unknown to the general public at the
time, a real space age instrument: the Fender
Stratocaster.

This instrument, designed and made in
California, dates from 1954, but solid body
guitars were not common then and most
musicians thought of them as a strange
novelty, a futile and superficial gadget, a fad
that would soon pass, just like rock 'n' roll
itself.

The early Stratocaster was nonetheless
an unsurpassable design classic. Its shape
became synonymous with the electric guitar,
even for beginners, and it remains completely
comfortable and functional sixty-three years
after its first appearance.

The two-tone sunburst finish (yellow and
brown, with no transition through orange,
unlike the three-tone sunbursts from the
1960s) and the maple fingerboard (which
was replaced with fine rosewood in 1959) are
shown to great effect on the sleeve of
the 1957 album *The "Chirping" Crickets*, which
includes the classic hits "That'll Be the Day"
and "Not Fade Away."

The first time most guitarists ever laid
eyes on a Strat was on this album sleeve, and
Holly is largely responsible for the
instrument's success. This image of him will
remain engraved in our minds for eternity, for
he was never to grow old: on February 3, 1959,
he was killed in a plane crash. He was just 22
years old.

DOUBLE-PAGE SPREAD
Buddy Holly's Strat reproduced
by the Fender Custom Shop,
face to face with the original
in the hands of its master.

THE CRICKETS
"That'll Be the Day"
The "Chirping" Crickets
(1957)

*The decoration on this J-45 ▶
is a tribute to Elvis
from Buddy Holly.*

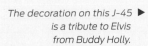

LEATHER

Buddy never took to the stage without his trusty Stratocaster. When it came to writing songs, however, his guitar of choice was an old Gibson, a simple model ready for any adventures. His J-45 is part of what is known as the Gibson "banner," a reference to the little flag at the top which proclaims, "Only A Gibson Is Good Enough." This flag can be found on all the Gibsons that were manufactured during the Second World War, guitars that officially don't even exist – since the factory that made them was supposed to be concentrating on meeting the needs of the war effort. These contraband instruments were made using whatever resources came to hand, and it was sometimes the case that the lack of raw materials forced the manufacturer to alter the specifications of its models. It can be seen for instance that Buddy Holly's J-45 has no space for a truss rod in the headstock, which means that it was made without this metallic reinforcement rod in the neck. Inspired by Elvis, Buddy made the leather housing for his J-45 himself. His name is therefore inscribed on it in the same place as Elvis's name on the Martin.

LES PAUL

THE BEST-SELLING SIGNATURE MODEL IN THE WORLD

▲ *Les Paul always considered the Les Paul Recording from the 1970s his favorite version of the model.*

THOUGH HiS GUiTAR WAS TO ACHiEVE GREATER FAME THAN HE EVER DiD, iT WOULD BE WRONG TO OVERLOOK THE ViTAL ROLE PLAYED BY LESTER WiLLiAM POLSFUSS, AKA LES PAUL, iN THE HiSTORY OF MUSiC.

This brilliant inventor was never happy with what already existed, and he was behind multi-track recording (the ability to record several different instruments on separate tracks) but also the solid body guitar (i.e. guitars that were not hollow). He conducted wide-ranging experiments in connection with the electrification of the instrument, as he sought the big, clear sound that he could hear in his mind. An essential stage of this quest was The Log, which can be considered the first solid body guitar in history. In 1940, he fitted two pickups and a vibrato arm that he had made himself to a piece of pinewood, and attached two wings taken from the body of an Epiphone archtop. He took his idea to Gibson at the time, but the company wasn't prepared to manufacture such a bizarre contraption in large quantities.

Everything changed in 1950, when Leo Fender released his Broadcaster, the first solid body guitar to be manufactured and sold on a large scale. Gibson sensed that they had missed an opportunity, so they called Les Paul back to design a model with him. Legend has it that Ted McCarty, president of the corporation at the time, played a substantial role in the origins of the design, a mahogany solid body with a sculpted maple top and a three-piece mahogany neck (far more sophisticated than Fender's rival model), a beautiful goldtop finish, and two P90 pickups. When the guitar came out in

1952, Les Paul had just released the hit "Tiger Rag" accompanied by his wife, the singer Mary Ford, and its success meant that he was a ubiquitous presence. The Les Paul wasn't the first signature guitar (Nick Lucas had his signature Gibson back in 1927), but it was the first to show the extent to which a name could be the making of an instrument. The Les Paul was to become such a huge success that it was later associated with a number of other legendary guitarists, and it therefore had other guitars modelled on it, which we might call "double signature" models, like the Les Paul Slash or Jimmy Page.

Les Paul in 1955, ▶ *accompanied by his wife Mary Ford and a greatly modified early Les Paul Goldtop.*

GRETSCH
CHET ATKINS
creating a standard

ENViOUS OF THE SUCCESS ENJOYED BY GiBSON AND iTS LES PAUL, THE GUiTAR MAKER GRETSCH DECiDED THAT iT TOO WOULD ASSOCiATE ONE OF iTS MODELS WiTH A GUiTARiST CURRENTLY iN VOGUE, in order to attract the hordes of young people who were falling for the instrument's charm. In 1954, Chet Atkins had just released his first successful instrumental single with "Mr. Sandman," making him the perfect ally. It was not easy to convince him (and he was to switch to a Gibson some years later, to see whether the grass was greener there), as he was lukewarm on the "western" decorations that Gretsch wanted to put on all his models (cacti, cows' heads...), far too "redneck" for a man who had been styling himself the Country Gentleman since 1953.

Just as with the Les Paul, it is not immediately clear which characteristics of the Chet Atkins model can be attributed to the musician rather than to Gretsch. The manufacturer was already making big guitars with a body fitted with DeArmond pickups before Atkins came along, the distinctive elements of the 6120 (the number given to the Chet Atkins) essentially being its orange color, its pickguard decorated with the musician's logo, and its Bigsby vibrato arm.

The guitarist's endorsement was a wonderful thing for Gretsch, though, and the model immediately became the maker's most iconic guitar. It was released in 1955, and two more versions were later rolled out: a model with a single pickup and a solid body

model. All three of them can be seen on the sleeve of the album *In 3 Dimensions*. Chet was a good partner and never missed an opportunity to promote his models.

He was also the inspiration for two further models: the Country Gentleman with a dual cutaway body in 1957 and the Tennessean, a cheaper version of the 6120, in 1958. These two guitars became classic models as well, but neither attained a status comparable to that of the unconquerable 6120.

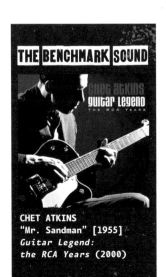

The modern-day Gretsch
6120, a timeless classic.
▼

The Chet Atkins features ▶
the horseshoe motif
typical of Gretsch guitars
on the headstock.

▲
Eddie Cochran posing with his Gretsch in the late 1950s.

EDDIE COCHRAN " C'mon Everybody " [1958]
Eddie Cochran (2015)

GRETSCH 6120
EDDIE COCHRAN
ADAPTING ONE'S TOOL

JUST LIKE BUDDY HOLLY, EDDIE COCHRAN WAS A SHOOTING STAR OF ROCKABILLY, AND IT WAS A CAR ACCIDENT THAT TRAGICALLY CUT SHORT THE LIFE OF THE WRITER OF "SUMMERTIME BLUES" and "C'mon Everybody" in 1960, when he was just 21 years old. He was discovered by the general public in late 1956, in the film *The Girl Can't Help It*, in which he plays "Twenty-Flight Rock" in a wonderful punk moment that was to be reprised by The Clash twenty years later. It is impossible to picture Cochran without also picturing his guitar, which he had modified so that it perfectly suited his needs.

His Gretsch 6120 was a Chet Atkins model typical of that time, with its beautiful orange color and its two simple DeArmond pickups. The refined and bright sound of the pickups didn't suit him in the neck position, so he replaced the neck pickup with a Gibson P90, much rounder and thicker. At the time, pickups weren't sold separately from guitars: to change them, players therefore had to take them from a different guitar which played the role of an organ donor, and this makes Cochran's sonic quest all the more admirable, since it was far from easy.
The second major modification that Cochran made to his Gretsch wasn't quite as visible but was even more significant.

The guitar strings from that era were enormous wound strings like telephone cables, perfect for jazz but very difficult to deal with if you wanted to bend the strings. Cochran wanted to play blues solos, so he

resorted to a famous bit of DIY: starting with a standard wound string, he put the *B* string in the *G* string position, thereby obtaining an unwound *G*, the *E* string in the *B* string position, and he used a banjo string for his high *E*. This deviation was later copied by string manufacturers and became the standard that is still in use today.

▲
The Eddie Cochran Gretsch recreates the modifications made by the singer himself.

TELECASTER
MUDDY WATERS
THE SCEPTER OF CHICAGO BLUES

◀ *Chicago's greatest bluesman, as inseparable from his Telecaster as ever, near the end of his life in 1979.*

MCKINLEY MORGANFIELD, BETTER KNOWN AS MUDDY WATERS, IS THE MAN WHO INVENTED THE SOUND OF CHICAGO BLUES WHILE BEING AMONG THE FIRST ARTISTS EVER SIGNED BY THE CHESS BROTHERS' LABEL. He wrote multiple classics of the genre, like "Mannish Boy," "Got My Mojo Working," "Rollin' Stone" (which influenced a certain little British band when it was looking for a name a few years later), and "Hoochie Coochie Man," all hits that helped to give him the most glittering career of all those who practiced this founding style.

Muddy was already playing the guitar when he lived on a plantation in the heart of Mississippi, but that was an acoustic guitar with huge, rusty strings, which he mostly played using the bottleneck technique, in the tradition of his mentor, Son House. He moved to Chicago in 1943 and gradually began to electrify his playing. First he was seen with a Les Paul Goldtop, then, in 1957, he bought the guitar that was to be his ultimate instrument, a blonde Fender Telecaster. The model's rustic solidity reminded him of the acoustics of his early days and he therefore felt perfectly at ease. Keen to stay current, he asked Fender for a new neck in 1961, when the maker was starting to offer necks with rosewood fingerboards, and he asked them to redo the color at the same time. Waters's famous red Telecaster with a rosewood fingerboard is therefore the same guitar as his blonde one with a maple fingerboard. Pretty amazing, right?

After a stint with Guild that was little more than a marketing operation, Waters never let go of his Tele again until his death in 1983; it then became the first guitar to have an exact replica of it made (right down to the smallest scratches) by the Fender Custom Shop, in 2000. Aside from its color, Waters' Telecaster is immediately recognizable thanks to an amusing detail: the two original knobs have been replaced with knobs from a Fender amp. The devil is in the detail.

DOUBLE-PAGE SPREAD
This ad from 1951 sings the praises of the new guitar from Fender, the Telecaster.

THE BENCHMARK SOUND

MUDDY WATERS
"Mannish Boy"
Hard Again (1977)

MICRO-ADJUSTABLE BRIDGE
Beneath snap-on cover. Three longitudinal screws for adjusting string length for proper noting.
Six elevating screws for adjusting height of each string.

ADJUSTABLE SOLO-LEAD PICKUP
Beneath snap-on cover. Completely adjustable for best tone-balance by means of three elevating screws.

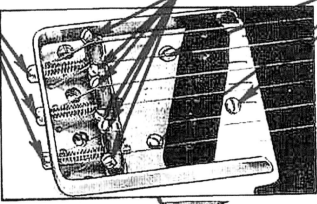

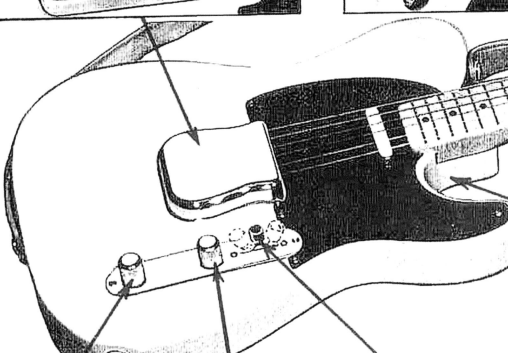

TONE-CONTROL
Functions as lead-pickup modifier in lead position of lever switch.

VOLUME-CONTROL
Functions in all positions of lever-switch and tone-control.

LEVER-SWITCH
Rear position for lead work modified by tone-control. Middle position for straight rhythm work. Forward position for deep soft rhythm.

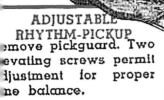

ADJUSTABLE RHYTHM-PICKUP
emove pickguard. Two
evating screws permit
djustment for proper
ne balance.

ADJUSTABLE NECK TRUSS-ROD
ove pickguard. Turn
ted cap-screw in end
neck to level frets.
que truss-rod design
kes adjustment sel-
necessary.

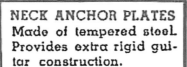

NECK ANCHOR PLATES
Made of tempered steel.
Provides extra rigid gui-
tar construction.

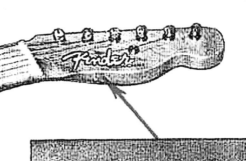

MODERN CUT-AWAY BODY
Permits easy convenience for
playing all twenty-one frets.
Thinner body makes playing
for long periods less tiring.

MODERN STYLED HEAD
Places keys all on one side for better access. Provides straight pull for
all strings.

RADIO & TELEVISION EQUIPMENT CO.

207 Oak Street
Santa Ana, California

"IF YOU TRIED TO GIVE ROCK 'N' ROLL ANOTHER NAME, YOU MIGHT CALL IT 'CHUCK BERRY.'"

JOHN LENNON

▲
This superb ES-355 recreates the specifications from the 1960s.

GIBSON ES-355
CHUCK BERRY
HAIL HAIL ROCK 'N' ROLL

"IF YOU TRIED TO GIVE ROCK 'N' ROLL ANOTHER NAME, YOU MIGHT CALL IT 'CHUCK BERRY.'" THIS JOHN LENNON QUOTE HAS BEEN USED EVERY WHICH WAY OVER THE YEARS, BUT THERE IS AN UNAVOIDABLE KERNEL OF TRUTH TO IT.
Chuck was the black Elvis and, unlike the latter, he wrote his own songs (including multiple classics such as "Johnny B. Goode" or "Roll Over Beethoven"), and he was a very gifted player of the electric guitar. His intros resonated like so many manifestos, his rhythm playing was solid and his solos were works of brilliance that later generations would try, and fail, to emulate (this led them to draw their own conclusions, like Keith Richards, who idolized Berry).

To attain this very distinctive sound, at once somber, piercing, and charged with electricity, he always used a Gibson thinline. Whereas most of the manufacturer's guitars, like the Gretsch and Epiphone guitars from that era, were semi-hollow and so very cumbersome and potentially sensitive to feedback, the thinlines appeared in 1955, just in time for Chuck to be one of the first to take advantage of their snappier sound. The Byrdland was at the high end, whereas the ES-350T was more suitable for thrifty musicians. Two years later, when Gibson started to use double humbucker pickups instead of P90s, Berry followed suit. Finally, in 1958, Gibson brought in the ES-335, the final model that pushed the logic of the thinline to its most extreme. Berry again

followed suit, and he was to remain faithful throughout his career to these perfect hybrids, whose dimensions corresponded perfectly to the maestro's on-stage acrobatics and the volume of the amps. He went through all the models in the range: 330, 335, 345, 355, and eventually opted for the latter, although Berry never became attached to one particular guitar. His instruments were merely tools with which to fulfill all his obligations, just like his accompanying musicians, whom he generally met just a few minutes before going on stage.

Chuck Berry kept on giving concerts well into his 80s, as evidenced by this poster dating from August 2010.
▼

GRETSCH
BO DIDDLEY
A SQUARE GUITAR, TO AVOID PLAYING IN THE ROUND

JUST LIKE CHUCK BERRY, BO DIDDLEY IS THE SOURCE OF A HUGE NUMBER OF CLASSIC ROCK STANDARDS SUCH AS "ROAD RUNNER," "WHO DO YOU LOVE," "I'm A Man," or "Before You Accuse Me." He is at the origin of a tribal rhythm derived from an Afro-Cuban clave, a beat dubbed the "jungle beat" or "Bo Diddley beat," used after him by artists as diverse as U2, Bruce Springsteen, David Bowie, and George Michael.

In addition to being an unparalleled composer, however, Bo Diddley was also a guitarist with an absolutely inimitable style, blessed with an impeccable sense of rhythm and an enormous sound, the result both of his use of open tunings and of his choice of material. He was one of the first to use the tremolo as a texture effect, but the most memorable things of all about him were his guitars.

In the middle of the 1950s, Ellas McDaniel (who had not yet acquired the nickname Bo Diddley) played a Gretsch Jet Firebird, the red version of the Duo Jet, but he already had the idea for a radical design, which he presented to the manufacturer. Faced with a lack of interest from the decision-makers at Gretsch, Bo made his rectangular guitars himself. In the great tradition of the instruments made from cigar boxes in the 19th century, he assembled his guitars by cobbling them together as best he could, and the resulting look was, of course, a lot more important than the sound he was able to get from them.

As they saw his growing success, Gretsch agreed to make the guitar that would go on to become the G6138 for him, a guitar that is still in the maker's current catalog and even acquired a cheaper model in the Electromatic G5810 series, proving just how innovative and durable Diddley's design was. He did not stop there, however: he also created the design for the Jupiter Thunderbird, rechristened the G6199 Billy Bo when Billy Gibbons gave it a makeover so that it would fit the fashions of the time, and the Duchess, which has not yet been re-released. Now listen up…

The Gretsch G5810, an affordable version of Bo Diddley's design, still available today.

Bo Diddley on stage in 1986. ▶ He is playing one of the square guitars that he built himself, a crude and original instrument.

THE BENCHMARK SOUND

BO DIDDLEY
"Bo Diddley"
Bo Diddley (1958)

LUCILLE
B.B. KING
THE KING'S QUEEN

IT'S HARD TO THINK OF A MORE EXPLICIT SYMBOL THAN GIVING YOUR GUITAR A WOMAN'S NAME. The most passionate guitarists are well aware of the extent to which the relationship you have with your six-string can resemble a marriage or a love affair: you share your deepest secrets with her, you protect her, you feel stronger when you're with her, and you can always rely on her. And then, of course, there are the curves that you caress lovingly in the dark corners of clubs in the wee small hours.

The bluesman B.B. King was from the generation that had known the desperate poverty of the cotton plantations; he grew up without electricity and spent his entire adolescence living alone. When he arrived in Memphis and began to make a name for himself as a radio presenter, he also gradually began to acquire the right guitars. Among them was an acoustic Gibson, and this was the guitar he was playing that fateful night in 1949 when everything changed. A brawl broke out in the club, the barrel of kerosene that was keeping the place warm was upended, and a fire quickly spread through the building. King emerged from the club unscathed, but realized he had left his guitar inside. Lacking the funds to buy himself a new one, he risked his life by running back into the flames to rescue his instrument. He later found out that the two men behind the accident had been fighting over a woman named Lucille, so he decided to name his guitar after her.

The name stuck and was used for all of B.B. King's subsequent guitars, and Lucille also provided the name for the 1968 album as well as *Lucille Talks Back* in 1975, and 1995's *Lucille & Friends*. The name became closely associated with a black Gibson ES-355 with no sound holes and a maple neck in 1980, when Gibson released the first Lucille model. Since then, Lucille has seen numerous variations in color and decoration, and is almost as well-known as her illustrious owner.

◀ *B.B. King at the start of the 1970s, when Lucille was not yet a mass-produced model.*

◀ *The current Lucille model, designed without sound holes and with a very distinctive bridge.*

THE BENCHMARK SOUND

B.B. KING "See That My Grave Is Kept Clean" *One Kind Favor* (2008)

THE BENCHMARK SOUND

Albert King

LIVE

69

ALBERT KING "Why Are You
So Mean To Me"
Live 69 (1969)

LUCY
ALBERT KING

WHEN A GIBSON IS NOT GOOD ENOUGH

ALBERT KING NEVER DID THINGS THE WAY EVERYONE ELSE DID. HE WAS A LEFT-HANDER, BUT PLAYED WITH THE STRINGS FITTED AS IF FOR A RIGHT-HANDER, with the treble strings at the top. And, what's more, he was among the very few guitarists who succumbed to the charms of the Gibson model that no one wanted. In 1958, the manufacturer Kalamazoo released the Flying V, and no guitarists dared to be seen holding it on stage in the spotlight...except for Albert King. The King stood a good six feet seven, and the V, which was a very wide guitar, suited him very nicely. The original V was a guitar made of korina, a wood whose sound is thinner and brighter than that of the mahogany traditionally used on the Gibson. King was no doubt sensitive to this sonic difference, which went beautifully with the very dry and finessed sound of his touch. He christened this guitar Lucy, inspired jointly by the comedienne Lucille Ball and by B.B. King, whose romance with his Lucille had gone swimmingly.

Gibson's slogan was "only a Gibson is good enough," but Albert King ended up expecting even more from his guitar, and he met the luthier Dan Erlewine. Erlewine made a walnut left-handed Flying V for him (so with the controls going in the right direction) with a headstock that was closer to the other Gibson models and with the name Lucy inlaid on the headstock and the bluesman's name written on the fingerboard. King must have liked the design, for he used nothing but this Lucy for a dozen years, before, in 1980, another luthier made a third Lucy fairly similar to Erlewine's creation, further proof of the affection in which he held this version.

At present, the first Lucy, the Gibson, is owned by the Hollywood actor and lover of beautiful guitars, Steven Seagal. According to him, King's ghost is never far away from his first great love.

◀ *Albert King with his original Flying V at the Newport Festival in 1970, before he replaced it with Lucy.*

LES PAUL SG CUSTOM
SISTER ROSETTA THARPE

SPREADING THE ELECTRIC WORD

THE GOSPEL GENRE IS, OF COURSE, NAMED AFTER THE GOSPELS IN THE BIBLE. SINGING GOSPEL MUSIC IS THUS ABOUT TELLING THE STORIES OF THE BIBLE SO AS BETTER TO SPREAD "THE WORD," something that no one did in such an electrifying manner as Rosetta Nubin, aka Sister Rosetta Tharpe. Nubin started out as an artist in 1920 when she was just 4 years old, singing and playing for evangelical churches. At the age of 23, she left for New York, where she would find fame by signing a record deal with Decca. Her high-energy interpretation of the gospel was not at all to the liking of the most traditionalist wing of the faithful, but others were entirely charmed, so much so that Tharpe was the only black woman to be asked to make records to maintain the troops' morale during the Second World War, and 25,000 fans were prepared to pay to be present at her third marriage in 1951, at a stadium in Washington, D.C.

Meanwhile, Tharpe experimented with a number of guitars before alighting on the right one. In the early days, she was often seen with a National Triolian, a guitar with a resonator (similar to a Dobro) which, at the time, made it possible to achieve greater volume than a standard acoustic guitar. She also appeared with a Gibson L-5 archtop, which, prior to the 1950s, came without a pickup. Tharpe managed to electrify her instrument, but as soon as a more convincing solution became available, she jumped at the chance to acquire it. In 1952, when the Les Paul was in its very first year of existence, she discovered the joys of the solid body and found the sound she was looking for, a sharp and brilliant electric shock. In 1961, sales of the Les Paul model had reached an all-time low, so Gibson replaced it with a new shape with a dual cutaway body, shaped like two little devil's horns. This new version of the Les Paul was rechristened the SG in 1963, and Tharpe set her sights on a white Custom, the most sumptuous version of all, with three pickups and a vibrato arm. This vision of this gospel singer wielding this ultra-modern guitar with an outrageous amount of talent is still striking more than half a century later.

THE BENCHMARK SOUND

ROSETTA THARPE
"Up Above My Head" [1948]
The Original Soul Sister
(2002)

Sister Rosetta Tharpe ▶
at a railroad station in Britain,
for the program "Blues and
Gospel Train" (1964).

5 ALBUMS WITH WHICH TO DISCOVER CHICAGO

CHICAGO BLUES IS THE ELECTRIFIED VERSION OF DELTA BLUES. IT EMERGED IN THE LATE 1940S, WHEN AFRICAN-AMERICANS FROM THE SOUTHERN UNITED STATES WERE MOVING TO THE NORTH TO FIND WORK AT THE STEEL FACTORIES. THE CITY INSPIRED THEM TO CREATE A MORE BRUTAL, URGENT, AND RHYTHMIC SOUND, WHICH WAS TO BECOME A SOURCE OF INSPIRATION FOR NUMEROUS LATER MOVEMENTS, NOTABLY THE BRITISH BLUES OF THE 1960S.

MUDDY WATERS, THE BEST OF MUDDY WATERS (1958) ▷

McKinley Morganfield, better known as Muddy Waters, was the most significant singer of Chicago blues. His dry, biting guitar notes complement a warm and authoritative voice, and this album brings together the best singles he released on the Chess label in the 1950s, his most exciting period.

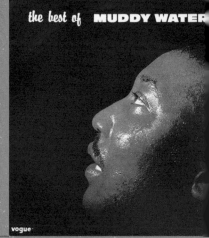

HOWLIN' WOLF, MOANIN' IN THE MOONLIGHT (1959) ▷

If you're going to give yourself a nickname like "howlin' wolf," you'd better make sure you've got the charisma to go with it — but charisma was never a problem for Howlin' Wolf. His physical presence alone would have been enough to make him worthy of the title, but his huge, husky voice provided all the convincing that was needed. The recordings from that time by this freak of nature are as fascinating today as ever.

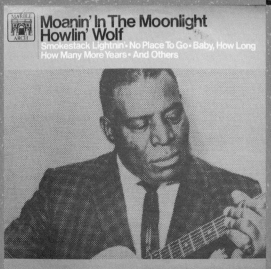

BO DIDDLEY, BO DIDDLEY (1958) ▶

Here again, this album is a compilation of the singles that came out earlier and represents the perfect introduction to Bo Diddley's unique groove. He is accompanied on it by the legendary Jerome Green, whose contribution to Bo's sound was of fundamental importance, and who plays an instrument that is definitely underrepresented in Chicago blues: the maracas.

◀ OTIS RUSH, RIGHT PLACE, WRONG TIME (1976)

This album came out in 1976, when Chicago blues had long since ceased to exist, but it was recorded in 1971 and represents the final pinnacle of the movement. Otis Rush sings and plays with a palpable sense of urgency; the band is four-square but not yet surgical, as rhythm sections in the 1970s would be able to be.

JUNIOR WELLS, HOODOO MAN BLUES (1965) ▶

He was one of Chicago's great harmonica players, and this first album perfectly captures the atmosphere of a packed club at around midnight on a Saturday night. On the guitar was an obscenely talented young guitarist, Buddy Guy, who also played with Muddy Waters at the time and who proves, on this album, that he already had a unique sound and playing style despite being all of 29 years old.

GIBSON ES-150
CHARLIE CHRISTIAN
JAZZ WITH YOUR FINGERS IN THE LIGHT SOCKET

CHARLIE CHRISTIAN JOINED BENNY GOODMAN'S ORCHESTRA IN 1939 AT THE AGE OF 23, THEN DIED OF TUBERCULOSIS JUST TWO-AND-A-HALF YEARS LATER.

Yet, despite this extremely brief career, he captured people's attention like no other guitarist through his role as a trailblazer, a pioneer, and the first real magician of electricity. Before Christian, the role of the guitar in the jazz orchestra was limited to strumming chords in every time signature, like the brilliant Freddie Green. The instrument wasn't strong enough to compete with the brass instruments in terms of volume, so its role was more percussive than melodic. The invention of the electric archtop guitar changed all that, even though in late 1936, when Gibson presented its ES-150, it was not an immediate success. The first version of Gibson's single-coil pickup was a hexagon with a metallic bar in its center, and it is currently known as the Charlie Christian pickup. In Goodman's orchestra, Christian used this new tool to bring out melodic lines and rich, complex solos that were ever so slightly saturated due to the limitations of the amps of the day. The influence of his brilliant playing, at the intersection of swing and blues, was felt by every guitarist that came after him.

▲
Charlie Christian with his ES-150 with a typical pickup.

THE BENCHMARK SOUND

CHARLIE CHRISTIAN
"Solo Flight" [1941]
The Genius Of the Electric Guitar (1990)

GIBSON L-5
WES MONTGOMERY
THE INCREDIBLE JAZZ GUITAR OF...

THE L-5 WAS DESIGNED IN 1922 BY GIBSON'S MASTER LUTHIER, LLOYD LOAR, AS THE GUITAR VERSION OF ITS A-5 AND F-5 MANDOLINS. This 5 series is now seen as the first golden age in the craftmanship of Kalamazoo, and, since the era in which it was created, the L-5 has cemented its reputation as the very best of what Gibson could do. This guitar with an archtop soundboard made of carved spruce was given a flame maple body and neck and an ebony fingerboard, signs of the special attention paid to the type of wood selected for each part.

Then the L-5 followed the fashions of the time and was given a cutaway body for better access to the treble strings, then one or two pickups (P90, then humbucker), so as to arrive at the current version, which is still the maker's top-of-the-line model and an ultimate luxury instrument.

No other guitarist mastered the L-5 quite like Wes Montgomery. This giant of jazz music had developed a very personal thumb-playing technique, and the gleam of the maple on the L-5 was the perfect complement to this naturally somber playing style. He used to say that he wasn't interested in the materials but, just as a master craftsman always chooses the tools he can rely on, Wes selected the things that Gibson did best and spent most of his life on this sunburst L-5.

◄ *Even today, the L-5 Wes Montgomery is still the most luxurious guitar produced by Gibson.*

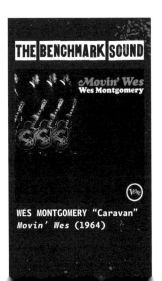

THE BENCHMARK SOUND

Movin' Wes
Wes Montgomery

WES MONTGOMERY "Caravan"
Movin' Wes (1964)

GIBSON SIGNATURE TRINI LOPEZ

FROM LATIN SURF TO HEAVY METAL

◀ *Trini Lopez
with his Custom model while
being filmed for TV in 1968.*

HIS NAME MAY BE NEARLY FORGOTTEN TODAY, BUT TRINIDAD LOPEZ — TRINI TO HIS FRIENDS — WAS AN ABSOLUTE SUPERSTAR IN 1960S AMERICA.

He represented both the voice of the Latinos who were starting to make a name for themselves in show business, and a version of rock 'n' roll that was acceptable to the younger generation's parents, such was the extent to which it was watered down and stripped of all adolescent aggression. It was the era when pop was thought of as no more than a passing fad, and a serious guitar maker like Gibson had no intention of getting involved with the electric stars who played their instruments. The artists who were entitled to Gibson signature models were therefore the big names in jazz, like Tal Farlow or Johnny Smith, or light entertainers for adults, like Les Paul. Trini Lopez undoubtedly

belonged in this second category, even though the two guitars that he designed show that he had far more imagination than his music.

His two models date from 1965, and share visual modifications that remain unique to Lopez: the headstock is extended, with six-on-a-side tuning machines (like on the Firebird), the fingerboard inlays are shaped like diamonds and, above all, so too are the sound holes, two rhombuses as opposed to the usual "F" shapes inherited from string quartet instrument making. The Custom had a deep body with two florentine (pointed) cutaways, whereas the Standard was a thinline with two rounded cutaways, effectively an ES-335 with Trini Lopez's typical decorations.

Thirty years later, Dave Grohl came across a Trini Standard in a guitar store while he was on tour with Nirvana, and fell in love with the instrument's look without knowing anything about the artist. It was the guitar that he would go on to use for all the albums created by his own pop-metal band, Foo Fighters, who became so popular that the Lopez was re-released as Dave Grohl's signature model by Gibson.

◀ *The Standard was
re-released by Gibson
and still resembles a
greatly modified ES-335.*

IBANEZ SIGNATURE
GEORGE BENSON
THE JAPANESE TAKE ON THE JAZZ GUITAR

GEORGE BENSON ENJOYED SUCH RESOUNDING TRIUMPH WITH HIS HITS "ON BROADWAY," "THIS MASQUERADE," AND "GIVE ME THE NIGHT" that it's easy to forget he was a guitarist before he became a singer. He was in fact one of the finest proponents of jazz guitar, the acclaimed heir to Wes Montgomery. What's more, his first album, released in 1964, was called *The New Boss Guitar Of George Benson*, a direct reference to the album by Wes released one year earlier, *Boss Guitar*. Moreover, he played a Gibson L-5, just like his mentor.

As its name definitely doesn't suggest, Ibanez is a Japanese guitar manufacturer. Originally, it specialized in making copies of Gibsons that were affordable but excellently crafted, and it was while testing one of its copies of the L-5 that Benson found out about the company's existence. After Gibson threatened to sue, Ibanez was forced to develop its own models and therefore set about searching for first-class artists with whom it could develop signature instruments. It made sense, therefore, for Ibanez to contact George Benson, who was already a true superstar in 1977, and, as luck would have it, he happened to be on the lookout for a

guitar that was easier to carry than a big Gibson, and less fragile from one gig to the next. An instrument that would be less subtle and precious than an L-5, but far more practical and durable.

Benson therefore gave the Japanese luthiers very specific instructions: he needed a smaller guitar, a scroll on the back of the neck for greater stability, an adjustable bridge so that he could alter the intonation settings easily, and two floating pickups so as to preserve the acoustic qualities of the soundboard without perforating it. A few months later, he was holding the GB10 in his hands, and, forty years later, this beauty is still in the Ibanez catalog — six different versions of it, in fact. Its success even extends far beyond the realm of jazz, for a guitarist like Prince made good use of it.

◀ *George Benson tests a prototype of his Ibanez guitar on stage in March 1977.*

GEORGE BENSON
"Just Another Sunday"
The New Boss Guitar Of George Benson (1964)

THE BENCHMARK SOUND

DJANGO REINHARDT
"Clouds"
The Last Studio Sessions
(1953)

SELMER
DJANGO REINHARDT
FRENCH DESIGN

Django Reinhardt was the main ambassador of the Selmer label, hence this ad from 1939. ▶

FRANCE DOESN'T HAVE A WHOLE LOT TO BOAST ABOUT WHEN IT COMES TO THE HISTORY OF ROCK AND THE GUITAR, BUT FOR ALL THAT, ONE OF THE MOST INFLUENTIAL GUITARISTS OF THE 20TH CENTURY was none other than Django Reinhardt (admittedly, he was Belgian, but it was in France where he built his career), a virtuoso whose undisputed good taste left its mark on both Jimi Hendrix and Brian Setzer. With only two good fingers on his left hand, he created a unique style for which he wrote the whole rulebook. Gypsy jazz has never quite been the same since it was lit up by the comet that was Django, despite the admirable efforts of brilliant musicians like Biréli Lagrène.

The guitar with which he is associated, which is also the one that the entire style was associated by extension, is the famous gypsy guitar, the Selmer. While it represents an evolution and extension of the classical guitar, the Selmer is in fact a distinct type of instrument, no less so than the electric guitar or the dobro, on which a specific repertoire is played. This instrument is the work of Mario Maccaferri, a guitarist and luthier who designed the flat cutaway body in 1932 for his classical guitars, distributed by the Selmer corporation. The manufacturer's main area of interest lay in brass and wind instruments. It was very much on trend when it came to jazz and therefore asked

Maccaferri for more volume and a brighter sound; he duly adapted his design so that it

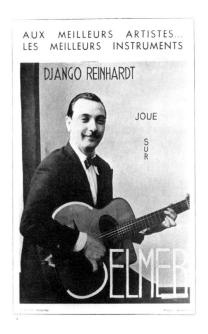

AUX MEILLEURS ARTISTES...
LES MEILLEURS INSTRUMENTS

DJANGO REINHARDT

JOUE

SUR

SELMER

could support steel strings. The Selmer-Maccaferri guitar was finally born in 1933. A year later, Django founded the "Quintette du Hot Club de France," the band in which the Selmer would become an icon. Django used several of them, for varying lengths of time: with his nomadic lifestyle, he wasn't the sort to grow deeply attached to material things. He went on tour in the United States in 1946 and was even seen with a Gibson archtop. He later experimented with the rough amplification typical of this era. Had he lived a little longer, just imagine the things he could have done with a Telecaster.

◀ *Django cheating on his Selmers, in the company of a Swedish archtop, the Levin Deluxe, during a concert in New York in 1946.*

THE BEATLES
Love...and a Lot of Guitars

THROUGHOUT THEIR RELATIVELY SHORT CAREER (FROM 1960 TO 1970, BROADLY SPEAKING), THE BEATLES NEVER STOPPED TRYING TO REINVIGORATE THEMSELVES BY SEEKING INSPIRATION wherever they could, from pop to jazz via heavy metal, serial music, and traditional Indian music. Their choices in guitars reflect this philosophy well, all the more so given that the Fab Four emerged at a time when manufacturers were constantly offering new tools, and often the Beatles were the first to use these new tools on a record, thereby defining the object in question forever afterwards. On top of this, if we take into account that the band included three guitarists (Paul McCartney was officially a bassist but he never turned down the chance to have a strum on the six-string in the studio), the list of instruments starts to get particularly impressive.

The band's early years in Hamburg and at the Cavern Club in Liverpool featured guitars whose elegant simplicity reflected their approach at the time. George Harrison played a Gretsch Duo Jet, and was to remain faithful

◀ The red Les Paul that Eric Clapton gave to George Harrison, the one he christened Lucy.

ARE YOU EXPERIENCED?

Numerous guitars reflect the Beatles' taste for experimentation, starting with the Rickenbacker 360-12, the prototype twelve-string electric guitar given to Harrison during their first tour of America in 1964. A few months later, it was at the heart of their sound on the album *A Hard Day's Night*. A classic Ramirez can be heard on "And I Love Her," a Tone Bender fuzz pedal on the bass in "Think For Yourself," a wah wah on "Across the Universe," a Fender Bass VI (a hybrid instrument, a cross between a guitar and a bass) played by Lennon in "Hey Jude," a Gibson SG for the riff in "Paperback Writer," and a prototype of the Fender Telecaster made entirely of rosewood is Harrison's chosen guitar for the recording of "Let It Be." Even their special guests play interesting and unusual guitars, like Eric Clapton, who joins them on "While My Guitar Gently Weeps" and to mark the occasion is given a Les Paul Goldtop, repainted in red and nicknamed Lucy, by Harrison.

George Harrison with ▶ his Gretsch Tennessean and John Lennon with his Rickenbacker 325 at the height of Beatlemania in October 1964.

to the guitar maker throughout the band's entire early period, before switching to a Country Gentleman, then a Tennessean. These instruments' characteristic twang can be heard very clearly in his solos from that time. As for Lennon, a Rickenbacker 325 was the object of his affections, a more unusual choice given its very diminutive size. The singer adapted it to suit his needs by adding a Bigsby vibrato arm and repainting it black, no doubt in a search more for the right look than for the right sound. Lennon, even more loyal than Harrison, went on to make it his main electric guitar, and then, in the years 1964 and 1965, he replaced it with another black 325 designed especially for him by Rickenbacker. It has to be said that, given the band's touring schedule, their instruments tended to age somewhat prematurely.

On the acoustic side, the band made a great deal of use of the Gibson J-160E, a sort of J-45 with a P90 at the base of the neck, a primitive form of acoustic-electric guitar that Lennon and Harrison used to plug into a Vox AC-30 amp, with very unusual results. McCartney's acoustic guitar on "Yesterday" was an Epiphone Texan (the Epiphone version of the J-45), and both Lennon and McCartney eventually fell for the Martin in the age of the double white.

During the second period, the look of their favorite instruments followed their state of mind: first they were decorated with psychedelic paintings at the height of their LSD period, then they were sanded down to get back to the raw wood when they became hippies, and were thus closer to nature. Lennon's Epiphone Casino underwent this treatment (the Casino is the Epiphone version of the ES-330, with no central beam and with two P90s, one of the band's favorites in their second period), as did his J-160E and McCartney's Rickenbacker 4001S bass guitar. Besides their guitars, the other thing we must sympathize for is their amps, because they had to try to make themselves heard over the raucous din of 55,000 screaming fans with some poor 30-watt Vox amps.

Hofner is still producing the Ignition Violin Bass today, and it's a good bet that most of those who buy it are fans of the Beatles.
▼

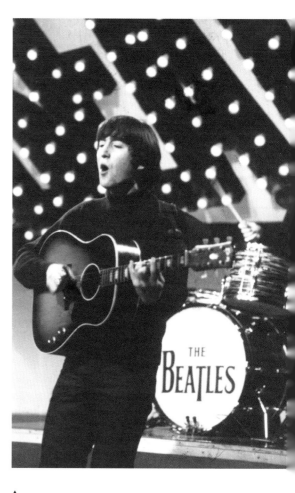

▲
One of Lennon's favorites, the Gibson J-160E that can be heard in many of the tracks from the early period.

John Lennon with his ▶ sanded Epiphone Casino in January 1969, during the band's last ever concert, on the roof of their record label's headquarters in London.

GIBSON FLYING V
Dave Davies
AN UNPRECEDENTED DESIGN FOR AN UNTAMED GUITARIST

TODAY, THE FLYING V IS ONE OF THE CLASSIC SHAPES FOR AN ELECTRIC GUITAR, TO THE EXTENT THAT IT HAS EVEN BECOME ONE OF THE UNIVERSAL SYMBOLS OF ROCK and is used as a logo for numerous bands, as well as stores and bars. When Gibson first unveiled this new model in 1958, however, the general public didn't know what to make of it at all. Just like its sister-model, the Explorer, which also had a very modern shape and was released in the same year, the Flying V did not sell well, and even though very few of them were made in the first instance (less than a hundred), they stayed in stock at the shops long after they were first released. Thus it was that Dave Davies, the lead guitarist of the band The Kinks, came across the V.

The Kinks were in the middle of a tour of America in 1965 when their equipment went missing between two flights, just before they were due to perform on live TV. Dave went to the nearest music store, but couldn't find a guitar that satisfied his requirements. It was then that he noticed an old guitar case in the corner of the room, and he immediately fell in love with what he found inside. Davies had

never even heard of the Flying V, but the dandy of British pop couldn't help but be seduced by its quirkiness. The Kinks typically loved to make their own rules, going so far as to rip the membrane of an amp's loudspeaker in order to achieve the distortion that is so instantly recognizable in the single "You Really Got Me."

Davies' extremely distinctive look, with his Flying V (which he played by putting his right arm between the two wings, adding another touch of the bizarre to the spectacle) immediately captured the public's attention, a fact which Gibson was quick to pick up on. Two years later, in 1967, the manufacturer released the very first re-edition in its history, a revised and corrected Flying V, which went on to enjoy considerably more success than its predecessor.

◄ The Kinks during a televised appearance: Dave Davies with the Flying V, left, and, on the far right, his brother Ray with a Telecaster.

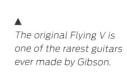

▲
The original Flying V is one of the rarest guitars ever made by Gibson.

THE ROLLING STONES
50 years and five strings

The Ronnie Wood L-5S was brought out by Gibson in 2015.
▼

THE ROLLING STONES' CAREER BEGAN IN 1962, AND, WITH THE EXCEPTION OF A BRIEF HIATUS IN THE 1980S, THE BAND HAS BEEN ON TOUR OR IN THE RECORDING STUDIO EVER SINCE. Add to that Keith Richards' fondness for collecting beautiful instruments, the three other guitarists who have been members of the band (Brian Jones, Mick Taylor, and Ron Wood, who has been with the Stones since 1975), and the fact that Jagger himself often likes to strum on a Gibson, a Silvertone, or a Taylor, and the result is a simply staggering collection of instruments.

We'll therefore limit ourselves here to Keith's most emblematic guitars. He is associated above all with the instrument that represents him, a 1953 Telecaster, featuring a butterscotch finish with a black pickguard, nicknamed Micawber after the character created by Charles Dickens. This was the guitar that he played with an open *G* tuning, and, to do so, he took off the low *E* string, which isn't particularly useful in this kind of tuning, to obtain a more direct resonance. The principle was simple: fewer notes, therefore greater efficiency — just like its owner's playing! Micawber was heavily modified: the neck pickup was replaced with a Gibson humbucker, the three-saddle bridge was replaced with a six-saddle one without the sixth saddle (as the guitar only had five strings), and the tuning machines were changed. A weapon that has stood the test of time, the guitar has been touring the world since 1970 with no let-up.

Always striving for simplicity, Richards has also made much use of a Les Paul Junior by Gibson, a model made entirely of mahogany (without an inserted top) with a single P90.

This model was launched in 1954 as a cheaper alternative to the more luxurious Goldtop, but good guitarists soon realized that the Junior's excellent sonic qualities meant that it wasn't just for beginners. The unpretentious aspect of these guitars is a beautiful portrayal of the minimalist approach adopted by the pirate Keith.

When the band was just starting out, he played a Harmony Meteor, an entry-level thinline guitar, then moved on to an Epiphone Casino before the Beatles had the same idea a few months later. He was also seen during the recording of *Beggars Banquet* with a superb black Les Paul Custom with three pickups and hand-painted decoration, a Flying V (which he played at Hyde Park in 1969), and a see-through Ampeg Dan Armstrong with a Plexiglass body.

On the most recent tours, Richards seems to have fallen for a black ES-355, no doubt a nod to the man who'd always been his mentor, Chuck Berry.

Keith Richards in 1989 ▶
with the famous five-string Telecaster, Micawber. Behind him is the Music Man Silhouette in the hands of Ron Wood.

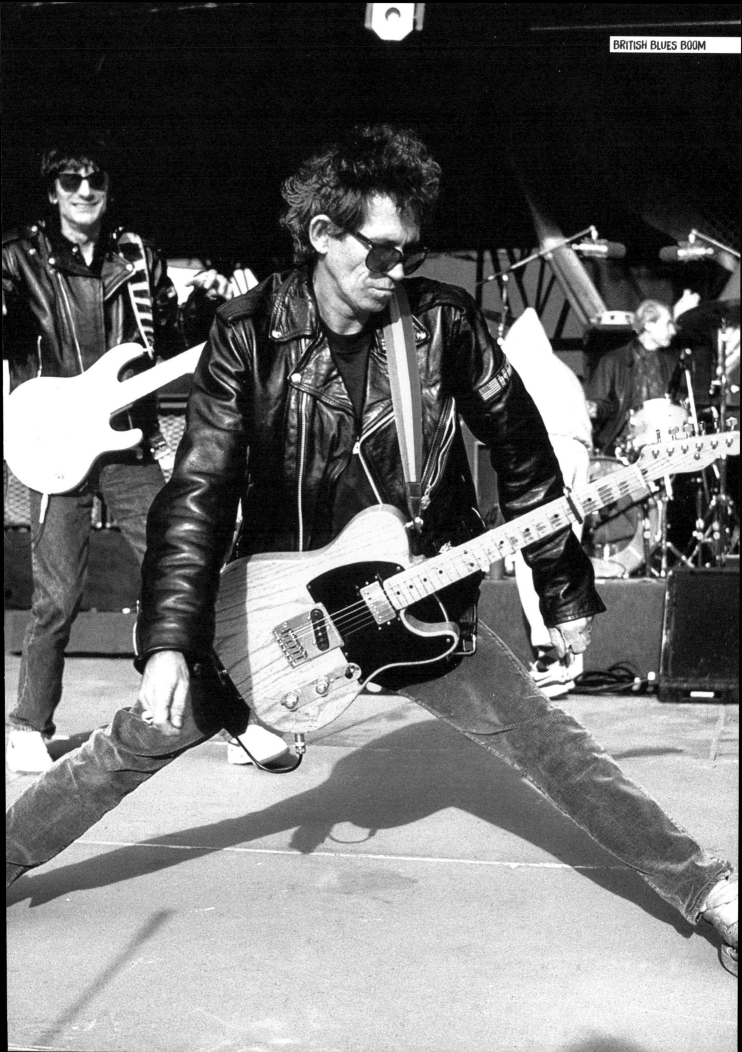

out of
our heads
THE ROLLING
STONES✴

THE ROLLING STONES
"(I Can't Get No)
Satisfaction"
Out Of Our Heads (1965)

THE STONES' BURST

For the band's famous appearance on the Ed Sullivan Show on American TV in late 1964, Keith Richards played a 1959 Les Paul Standard, a magnificent sunburst guitar modified with a Bigsby.

He was thus the first prominent musician to be seen with this model that was in production for just three years (from 1958 through 1960) and that no one wanted at the time. This Gibson was his main guitar for the subsequent tour (and so was probably the one used to record the immortal riff in "(I Can't Get No) Satisfaction"), before he moved on to something different and sold it in 1968. The buyer was the guitarist from John Mayall's band, The Bluesbreakers. A year later, the Stones were looking for a new guitarist to replace Brian Jones, and their choice fell on Mick Taylor, the famous buyer in question. The Burst was thus brought back to the Stones, but this time in the hands of a second guitarist.

◀ *The Rolling Stones in the middle of filming for a TV program in 1964, during the few months during which Keith used the famous Burst.*

GIBSON SG SPECIAL
PETE TOWNSHEND

FUTURES SACRIFICED

PETE TOWNSHEND IS THE SPECTACULAR GUITARIST OF THE BRITISH BAND THE WHO, AND THE MERE MENTION OF HIS NAME IS ENOUGH TO MAKE ANY GUITAR IN THE WORLD TREMBLE WITH FEAR: since the mid-1960s, each of his gigs has ended with a massacre, with the poor instrument being tossed around the stage and sent crashing into the loudspeakers, before being smashed to pieces on the floor. Given that Pete is a former art student, this can be seen as the expression both a taste for performance and of a punk attitude of detachment towards the tools of his trade. The whole thing began completely by accident, however. The band was playing one night in a room with a very low ceiling, and Townshend accidentally rammed the headstock of his guitar against the ceiling. He had been playing a frail Rickenbacker — a guitar known for its fragility — and the headstock broke; the crowd assumed the instrument had been sacrificed

voluntarily, and the band's stock immediately began to rise, to the point that The Who felt obliged to repeat the trick, this time in a somewhat more choreographed fashion. Townshend was a punk but he wasn't crazy: the guitars that he put to the sword were always chosen in advance. In the early days, it was generally a Fender Telecaster or Stratocaster, very solid instruments that were relatively easy to knock back into shape afterwards. He would play the Rickenbacker for the rest of the concert, and switch to the Fender at the climactic moment. In 1968, he discovered the joys of the Gibson SG Special, a version of the SG with two P90s rather than the usual humbuckers, then the Les Paul Deluxe, a Les Paul with mini-humbuckers. These versions, less expensive than the classic ones, were also perfect for being destroyed then reassembled, whereas he never took on stage the Gretsch 6120 that he used to record *Who's Next* in 1971: he was well aware that it wouldn't be possible to salvage it after subjecting it to such brutal treatment.

The SG Standard P90 from 2016, a modern version of the SG Special that Townshend used at the time.
▼

This photograph ▶ was used as a publicity shot for the double album The Kids Are Alright in 1979

BURST THE MOST EXPENSIVE GUITAR IN THE WORLD

IN 1958, GIBSON WAS STRUGGLING TO SELL ITS LES PAUL MODEL, WHICH HAD BEEN OUTSTRIPPED BY THE COOLER, MORE MODERN DESIGN OF THE NEW GUITARS MADE BY ITS RIVAL, FENDER, despite its introduction of new dual pickups in 1957 to replace the P90s. Gibson therefore decided to change the finish on its solid body model to give it a sunburst (fading from red to yellow), which would make it possible to admire the grain of the maple top through the lacquer. It was then given the name the Les Paul Standard. Success was not forthcoming, for in 1961, the Les Paul design was abandoned, in favor of the design that would later become known as the SG. In 2017, a Les Paul Standard from that era (a model later dubbed the Burst, short for sunburst) would sell for between $185,000 and $620,000, making it the most sought-after model among collectors. This extreme change of fortunes in terms of desirability can be put down to a combination of numerous factors:

◀ **The Burst represents the pinnacle of skill in the art on the part** of Gibson in this era, with the right woods, the right pickups, the right lines, and an irreplaceable know-how.

The Burst is associated with ▶ some of the greatest rock stars in the world. *Keith Richards was the first to display it to the wider public, followed by Eric Clapton in* The Bluesbreakers *and then Mike Bloomfield, Peter Green, Jimmy Page, Billy Gibbons, Paul Kossoff, Joe Perry and Brad Whitford (Aerosmith), Duane Allman, Gary Moore, Rick Nielsen (Cheap Trick), Slash, and Joe Bonamassa.*

Original Bursts are very rare: ▲ *only about 1,500 were made, during a three-year period.*

◄ *Every Burst is unique, for no two maple tops are the same, and the colors are* always different. Only one finish was available at the time, Cherry Sunburst, but they were not all strictly identical and, above all, the colors aged at different rates depending on the level of UV light to which they were exposed.

JIMMY PAGE
THE MASTER OF THE BURST

The Gibson Custom Shop ▶
Jimmy Page Number Two, a
perfect replica of the most
famous Les Paul ever.

JIMMY PAGE, A ONE-MAN EMBODIMENT OF THE FANTASY OF THE GUITAR HERO. NO OTHER MUSICIAN HAS ACHIEVED THE SAME BLEND OF MYSTERY, CHARISMA, SHEER TALENT, AND ENERGY, and his aura was only intensified by his refusal to sing in his band (not even on backing harmony!) and his routine absence from TV sets and other interviews. Fans of Led Zeppelin were therefore able to project whatever image they wanted onto this skinny young man with his unruly hair and dragon trousers, this image, of course, being distorted by rumors of wild sex, drugs, satanism, and black magic, rumors that Page, with all the shrewdness that Robert Johnson had once displayed, never troubled to dispel.

His choice of guitars was always in keeping with this character. Even when he played a Telecaster at the start of the band's career in 1969, it was a Telecaster that had been repainted by hand with a multicolored dragon pattern. This model with a rosewood fingerboard dates from 1959, a gift from Jeff Beck when Jimmy joined him in the band The Yardbirds. However, at the end of 1969, the Les Paul came along to replace the Tele as the band's emblematic instrument, like a fifth band member. It is said that few guitarists have done as much to showcase the thick and edgy sound of the Burst, as though Led Zeppelin's riffs had been written as a series of arguments in favor of this thing of beauty. His number one guitar, known, naturally, as Number One, is a 1959 model whose neck was sanded down to make it more slender and thus more suitable for Page's hands. The original tuning machines were also replaced with gold Grovers, to which Page had grown

accustomed since his days playing the Les Paul Custom on which he made his Session Man compilation in the 1960s. Jimmy also took off the cover of his bridge humbucker to gain some high notes, a modification that was to be copied by several generations of fans even though they couldn't really hear much of a difference.

Number Two was also a 1959 Les Paul (the Page legend goes a long way towards explaining the particular fondness that collectors have for this vintage over the ones from 1958 and 1960), slightly more somber than the Number One and modified in exactly the same way, with the added detail of some highly complicated electronics. Page fitted switches to it so that he could get fifteen different sounds from the two basic pickups, no doubt a habit acquired during his days as a session musician, when he had been expected to offer a variety of textures, a requirement that he was to retain as the captain of Led Zeppelin.

NEXT DOUBLE-PAGE SPREAD
Jimmy Page on stage
with his Les Paul, on 14
June 1977 in New York.

ALSO-RANS

The two Bursts may have enjoyed the lion's share of affection in the hearts of fans, but Page also called upon other instruments, both in the studio and on stage, so as to cover the widest possible range of sound. He made systematic use of a Danelectro DC59 for pieces played in open tuning such as "Kashmir" or "In My Time of Dying," thereby rendering desirable this cheap American guitar, made of plywood and with its feeble, nasal pickups (the famous lipstick pickups, so named because they were coiled inside tubes of lipstick retrieved by the Danelectro factory). He was also seen with a 1964 Stratocaster in the wonderful custom Lake Placid Blue color, and a Telecaster assembled using different parts. Finally, a single piece of music justified a different guitar all of its own, but not just any piece of music: the rock rhapsody "Stairway to Heaven" incorporates some parts played on a six-string and others played on an electric twelve-string (a Fender Electric XII in the studio), hence the use of the double twelve/six neck to reproduce this tour de force on stage. The famous Gibson EDS-1275, the double-neck SG, has since become a rock scepter par excellence, the ultimate stage prop and object of desire.

◀ *Few images sum up so well the grandeur of rock as that of Jimmy Page in his dragon print suit, armed with his dual-neck SG, in 1975.*

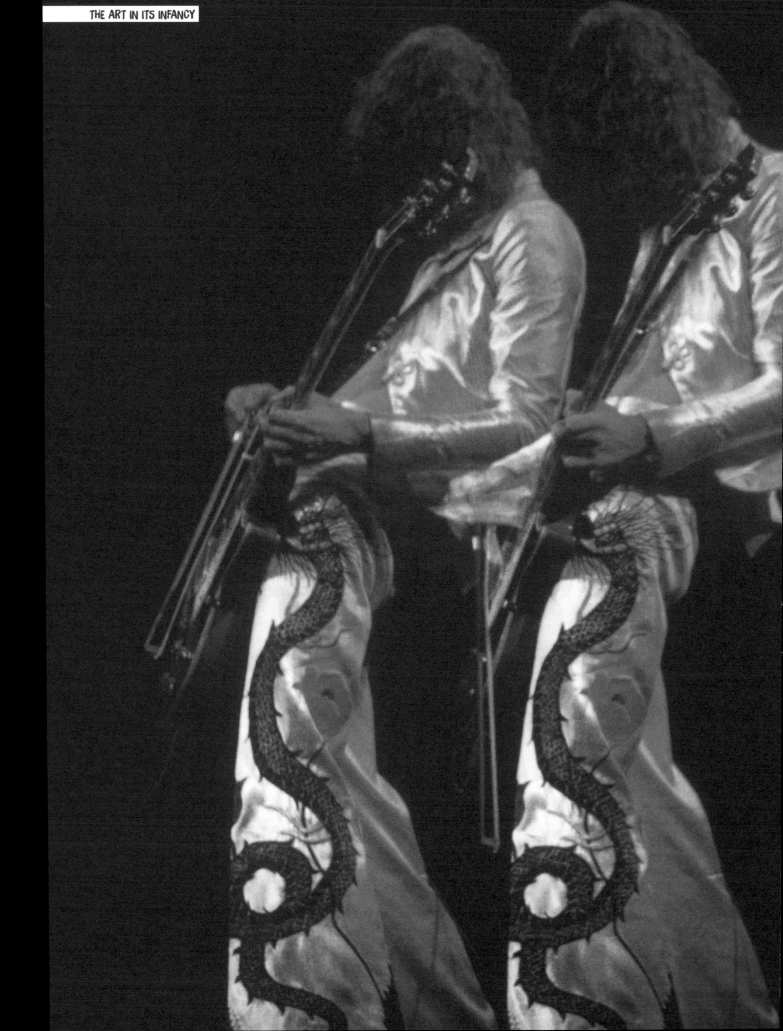

ERIC CLAPTON

DIVINE RELICS

NO OTHER GUITARIST HAS HAD HIS NAME ASSOCIATED WITH AS MANY SIGNATURE ELECTRIC GUITARS, ACOUSTIC GUITARS, AND AMPS AS ERIC CLAPTON.

There are several factors that explain this mania for all things Clapton: the considerable talent of the star of British Blues is, of course, part of the equation, but we also have to add in the insatiable thirst for equipment that led him to play an astronomical number of guitars over the course of his career, and finally there are the Clapton fans, baby boomers with plenty of disposable income, the perfect target audience for signature guitars, which can often sell for well over $12,000.

It has to be said that the man dubbed "God" in 1967 never stopped giving his admirers the wish to get a guitar. It is even fair to say that Clapton is partially responsible for the mania for vintage guitars, for he was among the first to argue the case for old

instruments. He played a 1960 Burst with John Mayall & the Bluesbreakers, and suddenly everyone wanted to get their hands on a Les Paul Standard. When that guitar was stolen, Clapton's emblematic guitar in the Cream trio became a Gibson SG, repainted with psychedelic patterns. Within a few months, there was not a guitar left in London that hadn't been repainted. In the 1960s, he also put in appearances with a red ES-335 and a Les Paul Goldtop repainted in red and nicknamed Lucy.

The 1970s arrived and Clapton reinvented himself as a solo artist. He moved from Gibson to Fender and performed with two Stratocasters, which became his special favorites. Brownie is a 1956 Strat featuring a two-tone starburst finish, with a well-worn maple fingerboard, proof, according to Clapton, of the guitar's quality. Blackie was assembled using parts from different guitars: a black body from 1956 and a neck with a maple fingerboard from 1957. It is the maestro's go-to weapon, and you can instantly recognize the snappy sound of the intermediate position, which combines bridge pickup with middle pickup, on his albums from the 1980s.

In 1988, Clapton became the second artist to have a signature Fender Stratocaster (the first was the Swedish virtuoso Yngwie Malmsteen). He recreated the shape of Blackie's V-neck and opted for a resolutely modern electronic sound. The Lace Sensor pickups make it possible to avoid the interference typical in vintage single-coil pickups, and an integrated active boost circuit enables him to manage his volume without the need for an additional pedal. A Custom Shop version was to follow, and the signature Clapton is still one of the bestselling items in the entire Fender catalog today.

In 2013, the Fender Custom Shop produced 100 replicas of the Stratocaster Brownie. ▼

Eric Clapton in 1990 ▶
with the signature Strat,
no doubt featuring one
or two cigarette burns
on the headstock.

THE WOODED SIDE

In 1992, the album *Unplugged* reminded the whole world in one go of the extent to which a good acoustic guitar can fill space without the need for cumbersome and complicated keyboards. On MTV's broadcast of the concert, Clapton is seen with a classic Ramirez guitar and a dobro. However, the show's main tool, which can also be admired on the album sleeve, is a 1939 Martin 000-42, a magnificent and highly desirable item whose medium-sized body makes it possible to obtain the snappy sound of the small guitars from the 1930s, typical of blues, while gaining a little more solidity in the bass notes. This appearance marked the start of what was to be an extremely productive collaboration between Eric Clapton and the great acoustic guitar manufacturer: nine limited edition models were produced between 1995 and 2014, and all of them sold out in a flash. The model with serial number 000-28EC is the simple and effective version of the Claptonian acoustic guitar, and even today it remains one of the most popular models in Martin's catalog.

The 000-42M was ▶ also a limited edition model (250 were made) with a Madagascar rosewood body, but featuring more luxurious decoration typical of the 42 series.

The 000-28M, a limited edition of Clapton's signature Martin that has the special feature of a body made of Madagascar rosewood.
▼

◄ *The original Martin that Clapton played for the recording of Unplugged, a 000-42 from 1939.*

BURST
PAUL KOSSOFF
THE GREATEST UNKNOWN GUITARIST OF ALL TIME

▲
Paul Kossoff on stage, in a pose typical of the hard rock of the 1970s.

IN AN IDEAL WORLD, FREE WOULD BE RECOGNIZED AS HAVING BEEN A TRULY GREAT HARD BLUES ACT, AND THE BAND'S GUITARIST, PAUL KOSSOFF, WOULD REGULARLY FEATURE AT THE TOP OF THE LISTS OF ALL-TIME GREATS compiled by the specialist magazines. Instead, the only thing most people remember about Free is their hit from 1970, "All Right Now," and Kossoff is seen as just one more British bluesman. Yet every note Kossoff plays is a genuine lesson in feeling, in the perfect mastery of vibrato, and in good taste, not to mention the smooth, round sound that he was able to get out of his Les Paul guitars. And he was still a legal minor when the band got together! As a huge fan of Clapton, he wanted a Les Paul, so he began his quest with an affordable Les Paul Junior before setting his sights on a black Custom guitar made in 1955. Before long, though, he realized that the Custom's P90s weren't allowing him to get the result he wanted, so he eventually found what he wanted with a sunburst Standard from 1960. Kossoff's life was chaotic to say the least, and he never held on to the same guitar for very long, to the extent that there were around four or five different Bursts that he owned at one time or another, one of which was sanded down while another had its headstock broken after being thrown in the air at the end of a concert.

BURST PETER GREEN

IN PHASE AND OUT OF PHASE

Peter Green in 1969 ▶
at his peak, in Fleetwood
Mac, protected by his
magnificent Burst.

JUST LIKE PAUL KOSSOFF, PETER GREEN FELL VICTIM TO A GREAT INJUSTICE ON THE PART OF POSTERITY, AS HIS COLOSSAL TALENT WAS NEVER REALLY GIVEN THE RECOGNITION IT WAS DUE.

He was part of John Mayall's Bluesbreakers, then helped to found Fleetwood Mac before developing his solo career, and, throughout all these adventures, the magnificent reedy and lyrical sound that came out of his guitar remained a constant.

The Les Paul on which Peter Green played through the early years of his career is, moreover, just as well-known as its former owner, if not more so. It was a 1959 Burst on which the pickups were out of phase. The source of this defect is debatable: it may have come about during assembly at the factory or as due to a modification, but the end result is the same: when two sources are out of phase, they cancel out certain frequencies and provide a more refined and hollow sound. The secret to Peter Green's sound was thus copied by numerous other guitarists, to the extent that his Les Paul was the first to be replicated, right down to the tiniest details, for Gibson's Collector's Choice series.

At the start of the 1970s, Green sold his Les Paul to Gary Moore, who spent a large portion of his career with it before yielding it to the collector Melvyn Franks, who recently sold it for an estimated two million dollars to Kirk Hammett, the guitarist for the band Metallica.

THE GOLDEN AGE

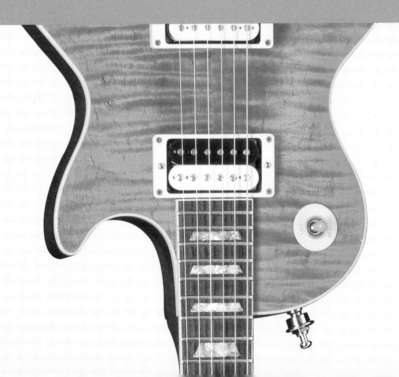

SURF, GARAGE ROCK, PSYCHEDELIA

86

THE BIRTH OF HARD ROCK

114

ARENA ROCK, SHRED AND NEW WAVE

138

STRATOCASTER
DICK DALE
THE SURFBOARD

DICK DALE IS THE UNCONTESTED KING OF SURF GUITAR, THE MAN WHO GOT CLOSER THAN ANYBODY ELSE TO RECREATING THE SOUND OF THE WAVES THROUGH THE HEAVY USE OF REVERB AND REPEATED ASSAULTS ON HIS STRATOCASTER.

His singles from the late 1950s and early 1960s remain true classics, which saw a significant resurgence in popularity after "Misirlou" was used by Quentin Tarantino on the original soundtrack for *Pulp Fiction*. Like Albert King, Dale is left-handed, but he learned to play on a right-handed guitar without reversing the strings, and this partially explains the sound he managed to achieve. Dale was a close friend of Leo Fender, so much so that Dale tested Fender's inventions and also suggested improvements and new functions that could be included in the maker's instruments. We have Dale to thank, in particular, for the Dual Showman, Fender's most powerful amp at the time, the baffles with their 15-inch JBL loudspeaker (oversized to encase the purring bass notes — Dale allegedly set fire to around fifty amps due to the volume at which he played, before arriving at a prototype that satisfied him), and the famous Fender Reverb Unit, the reverb box that is still the Holy Grail for any surf guitarist.

His guitar of choice was a Stratocaster with a rosewood fingerboard. It was seen in the 1950s with a white finish, but was later repainted in Chartreuse Sparkle, a golden color not unlike the color of champagne. The fact that he was playing a rosewood Strat in 1958, and perhaps even earlier, whereas the move to rosewood took place a year later on the models in this series, can, of course, be put down to his great friendship with Fender. He simplified the settings on his instrument by taking off the two tone controls, and above all he fitted the biggest strings possible to it, size 016-060. Suffice it to say that if you want to get anywhere near Dick Dale's sound, you're going to need to give your fingers a hefty workout.

The Signature Dick Dale. The Fender Custom Shop's Stratocaster recreates the great man's preferences and puts them within the public's reach. ▶

THE BENCHMARK SOUND

DICK DALE
"Misirlou" [1962]
*The Very Best
Of Dick Dale* (2010)

*Dick Dale in concert in the
1950s. He holds his guitar
like a left-hander, but
without having reversed
the strings, so with the bass
strings on the bottom.*
▼

STRATOCASTER Hank Marvin

THE MOST COVETED STRAT IN ENGLAND

▲
The signature Hank Marvin Fender Stratocaster, in red, needless to say.

EVEN THOUGH THE SHADOWS WERE INITIALLY THE BAND WHO ACCOMPANIED THE SINGER CLIFF RICHARD, THEIR INSTRUMENTAL HITS, SUCH AS "APACHE," TURNED THEM INTO STARS IN THEIR OWN RIGHT. The band's soloist, Hank Marvin, was the first British guitar hero, the idol who sowed the seeds of a desire to play guitar in many of the future heavyweights of rock. And more specifically: the idol who made them want to play a Stratocaster. In 1959, a prohibitive tax made it very difficult to bring American products onto British soil, and US guitars were therefore an extremely rare commodity in the country. Marvin was a fan of James Burton, Ricky Nelson's guitarist, and he wanted to have the same guitar as him. With information hard to come by, all he knew for sure was that his idol played a Fender. After seeing the sleeve of a Buddy Holly album and realizing that the Stratocaster was the manufacturer's number one guitar, Marvin placed an order. Thus it was that one of the most influential Strats of all time was ordered by mistake, because the instrument Burton played was, of course, a Telecaster.

The model that Marvin ordered was painted Fiesta Red, a custom color that was to remain forever associated with Hank Marvin, and featured gold appointments and a mottled maple neck, two rarities that only added to its appeal. At the end of 1963, Marvin was tempted away from his first love by the overtures of Burns, a British firm that endorsed the whole band on an exclusive basis. He was therefore entitled to a signature model that, when all was said and done, had specifications very similar to those of the Strat, to which he ultimately returned twelve years later when the contract with Burns was up. In 1986, the Californian guitar firm recognized the enormous role that Marvin had played in helping to popularize the Strat by giving him the second guitar ever manufactured after Fender was bought back by its staff.

Hank Marvin on stage ▶ in 2008, still cradling his red Strat at the age of 67.

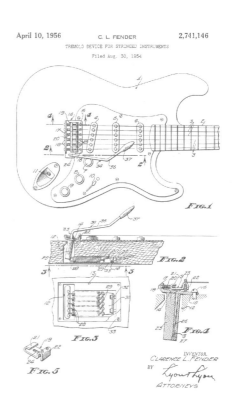

MOSRITE
THE VENTURES
MADE IN CALIFORNIA

SURF MUSIC IS AMERICAN MUSIC PAR EXCELLENCE, THE NEW WORLD'S CONTRIBUTION TO THE ROCK LANDSCAPE IN THE LATE 1950S AND EARLY 1960S.

Among the legends who sculpted this particular style, no one played a role as significant as that of the Ventures. With more than 110 million albums sold, the four musicians from Tacoma formed the instrumental band that enjoyed the greatest popular success in the history of rock. Like most surf musicians, the Ventures used guitars manufactured by Fender in California, but, in 1963, they became ambassadors for the firm Mosrite. These guitars, also made in California, were created by the designer Semie Moseley. The Ventures had their own models in the company's catalog, and all their albums stipulated that they played

Mosrites and nothing else. Given the band's incredible popularity at the time, it's not difficult to imagine that the publicity generated for Mosrite must have led to some hefty profits.

After the event, however, this publicity coup had a bitter after-taste of financial cynicism, because the moment their contract was up five years later, in 1968, the Ventures went back to playing their Stratocasters and Jazzmasters. Business is business.

THE VENTURES
"Walk Don't Run '64"
Walk, Don't Run Vol. 2
(1964)

Don Wilson with ▶
his Stratocaster and
Bob Bogle with his
Jazzmaster in 1961.

RICKENBACKER 360-12
ROGER McGUINN
THE RINGING TWELVE-STRING

ROGER MCGUINN WAS THE GUITARIST, SINGER, AND MAIN SONGWRITER FOR THE LOS ANGELES BAND THE BYRDS. HE WAS THE VISIONARY WHO GAVE THE BAND ITS VERY DISTINCTIVE and instantly recognizable sound, which bands like Tom Petty and The Heartbreakers or R.E.M. emulated. This native of Chicago was a huge fan of folk music and so knew his way around an acoustic twelve-string guitar. He was thus among the first to show interest in the electric version launched by Rickenbacker in 1964.

The Byrds recorded their first single in 1965, when McGuinn finally found the sound he was looking for. The problem with his Rickenbacker was that it had a very short sustain. The sound engineer for the recording session put a compressor on the tracks, as is often the case in the studio, and McGuinn

was stunned: the effect, configured with the settings turned up to the max, gave his notes the desired length, and on top of that brought out the sparkle of the treble strings, perfectly illustrating the expression from the chorus of "Mr. Tambourine Man": "in the jingle jangle morning." What could have been just one more version of a Bob Dylan song instantly became the sound of a new generation.

Roger McGuinn's Rickenbacker 360-12.
▼

STRATOCASTER
JIMI HENDRIX

A BONFIRE IN MONTEREY

JIMI HENDRIX REMAINS TO THIS DAY THE GUITAR HERO TO END ALL GUITAR HEROES, THE ONE EVERYONE WANTED TO IMITATE (just take a look at Clapton's afro hairstyle in 1967) but who remains untouchable, whose sound and feel simply cannot be reduced to the caricatures created by Robin Trower, Stevie Ray Vaughan, or Eric Gales. Jimi was a pure product of Flower Power, an iconoclast whose indifference to the material side of things comes across clearly in his relationship to the instrument. His career was all too brief: though he played professionally from 1963 onwards, his first recording dates from 1967 (the excellent *Are You Experienced*) and he died in 1970 at the age of 27. In the space of just three years, he was seen with a mightily impressive number of guitars. For different concerts and recordings, he can be heard on a Jazzmaster, a Les Paul Custom, a Flying V, and an SG Custom, and he didn't hesitate to borrow his friends' guitars when he needed them. For example, he borrowed a Telecaster belonging to Mitch Mitchell, his bassist, to record "Purple Haze."

The guitar with which he will forever be associated, however, and rightly so, is the Stratocaster. Other musicians had made the instrument their own before him, but none had taken Leo Fender's brilliant invention as far as he did. In Hendrix's hands, the Strat became an electric horse capable of producing the most beautiful and savage sounds. Not one to indulge in nostalgia for vintage models, he always played new or recently made guitars and was to change Strats as often as he changed his stage outfits. He didn't have a favorite among them, his talent staying at exactly the same stratospheric level regardless of which model he happened to be wielding.

The only trace of romanticism in his relationship to the Strat can be found in his shamanistic treatment of a pair of sacrificial victims. In 1967, he was playing at London's Saville Theatre (this concert became famous as the one in which he covered The Beatles' "Sergeant Pepper," released three days earlier) and the Strat on which he finished the concert had flowers, arabesques, and words painted all over it. The poem written by Hendrix is a dedication to the guitar itself, which ended up smashed to pieces on the floor at the end of the show. Less than a month later, Jimi produced another victim painted in a similar way at the Monterey Festival, but, knowing that The Who were on the billing too and that they also destroyed their equipment, Hendrix outdid them by going even further: he set fire to his guitar, in a magnificent bonfire that instantly took its place in the history of rock.

NEXT DOUBLE-PAGE SPREAD
On stage at the Monterey Festival, June 18, 1967.

Jimi Hendrix surrounded ▶
by the rhythm section of
The Experience in December
1967, at the Olympia.

THE BENCHMARK SOUND

JIMI HENDRIX
"Foxy Lady" [1967]
Jimi Plays Monterey
(1986)

MONTEREY POP

jimi
hendrix
he who
simon
& garfunkel
otis redding
janis joplin
he jefferson
airplane

THE LIMELIGHT

In 1968, Hendrix shared top billing for the Miami Pop Festival with a group of luminaries from San Francisco called The Mothers of Invention. Their guitarist, Frank Zappa, befriended one of Jimi's roadies, Howard Parker, and Parker gifted him a Strat that the great master had set fire to on stage. The neck and the electronics were largely intact, but the guitar's body had retained a fascinating hue of sunburst in flames, and Zappa therefore kept the body as a decorative touch. He later decided to attach a neck, a pickguard, and new pickups to it in order to turn it into a serviceable guitar, with which he posed proudly on the cover of the magazine *Guitar Player* in 1977.

> "MY DARLING GUITAR, PLEASE REST IN PEACE. AMEN."

◀ On stage at the Monterey Festival, 18 June 1967.

The Gibson SG Roxy, a re-release of the master's guitar. ▶

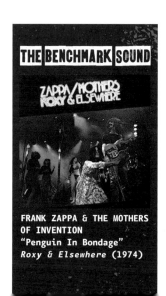

THE BENCHMARK SOUND

FRANK ZAPPA & THE MOTHERS OF INVENTION
"Penguin In Bondage"
Roxy & Elsewhere (1974)

GIBSON SG
FRANK ZAPPA
THE MOTHER OF INVENTION

Frank Zappa ▶ in a get-up typical of the "freak" movement, in the process of tuning the SG Roxy.

THE TERM "GENIUS" IS BANDIED ABOUT SO CASUALLY NOWADAYS THAT WE COULD ALMOST FORGET WHO THE REAL GENIUSES ARE, THOSE ARTISTS WHO THINK IN A RADICALLY DIFFERENT WAY FROM THE REST OF US MERE MORTALS.

Frank Zappa was a genius in many different guises, at once sound engineer, songwriter, singer, guitarist, band leader, and talent scout. No fewer than a hundred records were released bearing his name, in radically different styles, and his archives have not yet yielded up all their secrets.

As a guitarist, Zappa started out on Gibson jazz guitars in his band The Mothers of Invention, then moved on to an SG, a model he was one the few to defend, before switching to a Les Paul and heavily altered Stratocasters. He was always quick to apply his knowledge and experience as a sound engineer to his instruments. None of the guitars he used during a significant chunk of his career stayed in its original form — they were all subjected to a bit of soldering by their master at some time or other. Among the changes made were switches that could reverse the phase of the pickups, an XLR output (a format that engineers found preferable to the jack), integrated effects, active boosts with onboard EQ to control the feedback in an ultra-precise way, and even a twenty-third fret on the neck of the SG, which can be seen in the film *Baby Snakes*.

In 2013, Gibson came out with a re-release of the SG that Zappa played in 1974 for the concert filmed at the Roxy, with two small switches for phase reversal and pickup splitting. But this SG continued to evolve as Zappa's music progressed, and true fans had no doubt already fiddled with the electronics on their personal models.

LES PAUL CUSTOM
ROBERT FRIPP

THE LES PAUL REINVENTED

ROBERT FRIPP WAS NEVER THE SORT TO GO OUT HOWLING WITH WOLVES. HIS BAND, KING CRIMSON, REDEFINED PROGRESSIVE BRITISH ROCK WHILE CHEERFULLY EXPERIMENTING with jazz, proto-metal and avant-garde. To hear the great master's ultra-fluid guitar lines, the instrument almost sounds like a cross between a brass instrument and a synthesizer. And yet his equipment in the late 1960s was as classic as it gets: A 1959 Gibson Les Paul Custom (the famous Black Beauty), fuzz pedal and Marshall amp. It was a configuration that was then very widespread among British blues guitarists, almost identical to Jimmy Page's arsenal, for example. Such is the radical difference in sound between Fripp and Page that it provides irrefutable proof that a musician's fingers matter much more than the material he uses. It also provides further proof, if any were needed, of the brilliant design of the Les Paul, which today continues to be the perfect tool for musical styles that didn't even exist at the time it was invented. Robert Fripp went through a very large number of guitars during the course of his fifty-year career, but always came back to the Les Paul.

▲
Robert Fripp in 1972, just before the release of Larks' Tongues In Aspic.

PAUL REED SMITH
Santana
supernatural

CARLOS SANTANA IS AN EXAMPLE OF THAT RARE BREED OF MUSICIAN WHO FOUND THE SOUND HE WANTED IN THE MIDDLE OF HIS CAREER. Whereas most legendary guitarists had already found their texture when their first big opus came out, he fumbled around from album to album, eventually arriving at the sound that today is still instantly recognizable as his. His first appearance in front of a large audience took place at Woodstock in 1969, and he was sporting a Gibson SG Special, a model whose two P90 pickups produce a brilliant, dry, and aggressive sound. Two years later, he moved on to a Les Paul Standard for a thicker texture, and at the same time he moved from a Fender Twin amp (also very dry and brilliant) to a Fender Princeton, heavily modified by Randall Smith. It was while trying this amp that Santana came out with the line "this amp can really boogie," one that was later used by the maker to name his company: Mesa Boogie.

In 1977, he became the ambassador for Yamaha's SG2000, their version of the Les Paul (mahogany body, maple top, three-piece neck with two strips of mahogany flanking the main one of maple, and two humbuckers), with a dual cutaway body, then fell in love with the guitars made by the luthier Paul Reed Smith, who was just starting out at the time. He became the first artist to receive a signature PRS and even now is the manufacturer's best sales rep. The combination of PRS and Mesa Boogie still works today, for a sound that is round, warm, and very sensual.

◀ *Even those with small budgets can get their hands on their Santana signature model, as is the case with this PRS Santana SE.*

THE BENCHMARK SOUND

GUITAR HEAVEN
THE GREATEST GUITAR CLASSICS OF ALL TIME

SANTANA "Soul Sacrifice"
Santana (1969)

99

TIGER
JERRY GARCIA

A TIGER TAMED TO PERFECTION

◄ *The inlay that gave the famous Tiger its name.*

JERRY GARCIA WAS THE SOMEWHAT RELUCTANT LEADER OF THE HIPPIE BAND THE GRATEFUL DEAD, A BAND HAILING FROM THE SAN FRANCISCO OF THE LATE 1960S, the very epicenter of psychedelia. Garcia was known for his tremendous talent as an improviser, creating solos that could last thirty to forty minutes or more to punctuate the band's fluid concerts. He therefore needed an inspiring guitar, capable of following him on even his most outlandish ideas, but one also able to deliver varied textures so that audiences wouldn't get bored. Right from the start, therefore, Garcia was interested in his guitar's electrics, and he experimented with all their different effects over the course of his career.

It was this curiosity that led him to work with the Alembic studio in 1969. The firm came into being in the rehearsal studio of The Grateful Dead, then grew and grew until it eventually became a benchmark in very high-end basses, one that is still active today. In 1972, Garcia met Doug Irwin, a luthier who made guitars for Alembic, initiating a relationship of trust that had a rare intensity. The first guitar that he made for him, nicknamed Wolf in reference to the wolf

sticker with which Garcia decorated it, was a good starting point, but the ultimate guitar, the one in which the joint vision of the luthier and the guitarist was fully realized, was the Tiger. Commissioned when Garcia received Wolf in 1973, it took six years to make, weighed more than 13 pounds, combined numerous precious woods, and had an electronics system incorporating a preamplifier and effects loop.

Garcia was to have two more significant guitars, Rosebud in 1990 and then Lightning Bolt in 1993, both very similar to Tiger, which he played, incidentally, at his final concert in 1995. Tiger was auctioned in 2002 for $850,000 to the owner of an American football team, who put it back to work by lending the guitar to Warren Haynes for a tribute concert to Garcia in 2016.

◄ *Tiger in all its glory.*

THE BENCHMARK SOUND

GRATEFUL DEAD "Ripple"
American Beauty (1970)

STRATOCASTER
DAVID GILMOUR
THE BLACK STRAT

THE STORY OF PINK FLOYD IS A COMPLEX ONE, MADE OF POWER STRUGGLES AND TRAGEDIES. IT ALL BEGAN IN 1965, AROUND THE WEIRD AND WONDERFUL CHARACTER THAT WAS SYD BARRETT, who would never quite recover from the chemical experimentations in which he indulged.

In 1968, he was replaced by David Gilmour, a guitarist with a distinctly more bluesy playing style than that of his predecessor, and thus began the struggle with the bassist Roger Waters to determine who was going to take over the artistic reins. In 1977, Waters wrote *Animals*, then *The Wall* (1979) and *The Final Cut* (1981), with very little assistance from Gilmour. The band imploded but then Gilmour reformed it, without Waters, who was now concentrating on his solo career.

Throughout this tumultuous career, Gilmour remained faithful to the guitar that made him famous: the Stratocaster. Having grown up listening to Hank Marvin, he had always coveted a Strat, and a very distinctive model was to be at his side for many years. As can be seen by the constant upgrades to the amps and pedals he used, Gilmour was truly a man on a quest to find a sound, no doubt seeking a texture that he never quite fully discovered, staying on top of all technological advances in the hope that they might help him get closer to this goal.

The guitar known as The Black Strat bore the brunt of this research. Its life began in 1970, when David Gilmour bought a black Strat at the guitar shop Manny's in New York, to replace one that had been stolen from the band's truck six months earlier. The new one was a 1969 model with a large headstock and a maple fingerboard. In 1971, Gilmour replaced the volume knob so as to create the feel of a different guitar with easier handling. It was in this condition that the Black Strat was used during the concert in Pompeii. He also added an XLR output in a cavity that he filled in again very quickly after changing his mind, and replaced the tuning machines. In 1972, he subjected it to the first of a long series of changes of neck, swapping its neck for that of his sunburst model from 1963 with its rosewood fingerboard. He also added a switch that enabled him to activate the neck pickup in all positions, then bought another black Strat and transferred its electrics to the Black Strat.

In 1973, he fitted a humbucker pickup in the bridge position, making a cavity to house it as he did so, then changed his mind and put the single-coil one back in. One year later, he replaced the original white pickguard with a black one, then made himself a pioneer of replacement pickups by fitting a DiMarzio FS-1 in the bridge position.

In 1979, a Seymour Duncan took its place. In the meantime, the luthier Wayne Charvel had made a replacement neck for him, with a maple fingerboard. This was the beginning of the golden age of detachable parts and "Frankenstein" guitars. In 1982, the Black Strat

PINK
FLOYD
THE
WALL

PINK FLOYD
"Comfortably Numb"
The Wall (1979)

▲
*The Relic version of the
Custom Shop David Gilmour
Signature Stratocaster.*

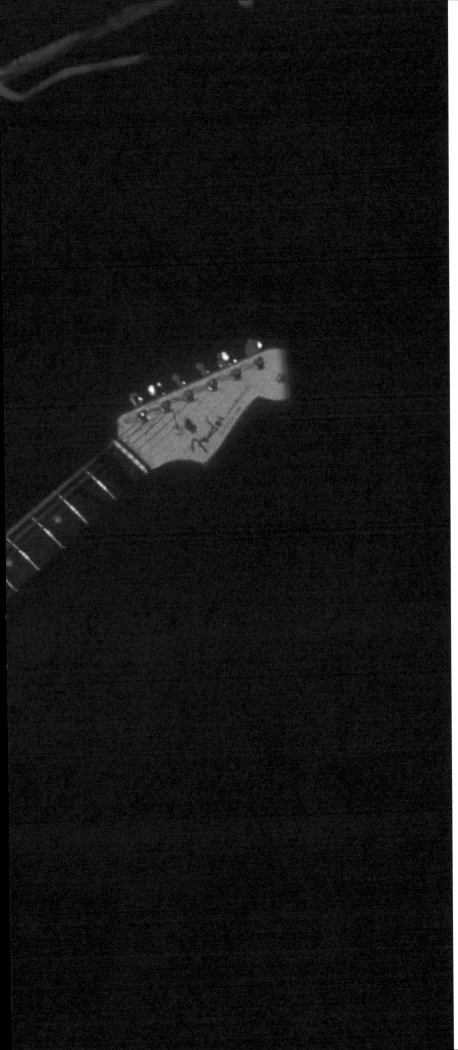

was given another Charvel neck, fitted with twenty-two frets rather than twenty-one, then its body was hollowed out again, this time to make room for a Kahler vibrato arm.

In 1984, David Gilmour moved on to Fender's new model, a re-release of a guitar from 1957, to which he fitted active EMG pickups. The Black Strat was lent to the Hard Rock Cafe, to decorate the walls of its restaurants. In 1997, Gilmour decided to get it back, and put a vintage Fender vibrato arm on it, along with a new neck, the one from the 1957 re-releases that he had gotten used to in the meantime. In 2003, he started playing it regularly again as part of the events marking the 30th anniversary of *Dark Side of the Moon*, then fitted it with another neck from a 1957 re-release, one that he found even more comfortable. The frets soon got worn down and so he changed the neck again in 2005. In 2006, the Black Strat appeared on the DVD cover of the concert at the Royal Albert Hall, then in 2009 the Fender Custom Shop finally came to measure it from every angle so that they could make a replica, recreating even the awkward details such as the traces left by the re-filled cavities around the vibrato arm and the XLR output. After getting through no fewer than seven necks and five pickup configurations, Gilmour finally seems to be content with the Black Strat in its current condition, but he no doubt keeps the soldering iron somewhere close at hand.

◀ *David Gilmour in 1977 on stage at Wembley for the filming of "In the Flesh."*

5 OF THE RAREST AMPS

GUITARS AREN'T THE ONLY THINGS THAT MUSICIANS COVET. AMPS CAN BECOME OBJECTS OF DESIRE TOO, AS AN EFFECT BOTH OF THEIR RARITY AND OF THEIR ASSOCIATION WITH ARTISTS IN THE PUBLIC EYE. HERE ARE THE FIVE AMPS MOST LIKELY TO GET YOUR GUITAR-PLAYING PALS SALIVATING.

DUMBLE OVERDRIVE SPECIAL ▶

Howard Alexander Dumble began his career by modifying Fender combos before starting to offer amps of his own, which worked well for Robben Ford, Stevie Ray Vaughan, Santana, Eric Johnson, and many others. In total, he made almost three hundred amps from the late 1970s onwards at his workshop in California, and when one of them turns up on the second-hand market, you need to have around $30,000 to $75,000 in the bank to have any chance of being its next owner. These stratospheric prices explain the abundance of clones that have been produced by firms like Two-Rock and Fuchs.

RAY BUTTS ECHOSONIC

Ray Butts was an inventor and engineer, a friend of Sam Phillips and Chet Atkins, whom we have to thank for the first version of the humbucker pickup. He is also the man behind the Echosonic amp, the first to feature a built-in tape echo effect. This brilliant option enabled guitarists to use a slapback delay on their live sound, whereas in the past this effect had been added later by a sound engineer in the studio. Chet Atkins purchased his in 1954, and, the following year, Scotty Moore made it his amp of choice after having first used it while recording "Mystery Train" with Elvis. Butts built approximately seventy amps, meaning that they are now nearly impossible to find. ▼

FENDER HIGH-POWERED TWIN

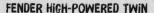

The Twin, with its two 12-inch speakers, has always been the most powerful amp that Fender ever produced. On its launch in 1953, that meant that it boasted 25 watts, but in 1958, it achieved the dizzy heights of 80 watts, a level of performance unprecedented at the time. This version, dubbed "high-powered" for obvious reasons, took two years to make and remains the favorite amp of true enthusiasts. It was the amp used by Buddy Holly and the guitarist of Gene Vincent and his Blue Caps, and today the likes of Keith Richards and Joe Bonamassa still swear by it. ▼

FENDER TOBACCO BARN TONE MONSTER

In 2016, Fender procured some extremely dry wood from a barn used to dry out tobacco in the late 19ᵗʰ century. Artists from the Custom Shop then designed an amp that would get the best out of these superb pieces of wood by making them resonate as they should do. Thus it was that the Tobacco Barn Tone Monster was born, featuring a Tweed Deluxe circuit with a 15-inch speaker, for a thicker, muddier sound than the standard 12-inch speaker. Only five units were ever built, and the tiny handful of musicians lucky enough to have used them won't forget the experience in a hurry.

◄ TRAINWRECK

Trainwreck amps were created by Ken Fischer, who started out creating parts to modify the amps of Eddie Van Halen and Mark Knopfler. In 1983, he made his company's first amp at his workshop in New Jersey, a supercharged version of a Vox AC30. Ever since then, rare Trainwreck models have always been given a woman's name instead of a mere serial number, and can fetch between $15,000 and $30,000 when sold. Fischer died in 2006 and so every genuine Trainwreck that will ever exist has already been made.

107

COODERCASTER
RY COODER
THE SLIDE MACHINE

TO CONFINE DISCUSSION OF RY COODER
TO HIS ROLE AS A GUITARIST WOULD BE
LIKE SAYING THAT LEONARDO DA VINCI
WAS A PAINTER: IT WOULD CERTAINLY BE
TRUE, BUT IT WOULD ONLY DESCRIBE AN
INFINITESIMAL PART OF THE MAN'S
TALENT.

At the very start of his career, he played on
the first album by Captain Beefheart, recorded
the haunting guitar music in "Sister Morphine"
for the Rolling Stones, then released his first,
eponymous solo album in 1970.

On this album, we discover his very deep
and wide understanding of folk music and his
mastery of the mandolin and bass (he was to
prove ridiculously talented on multiple
stringed instruments as his career progressed
and more albums came out), but above all
a bottleneck playing style worthy of the
greatest bluesmen of the Mississippi Delta.
When it came to electric guitars, Cooder's
instrument of choice has always been the
Stratocaster, no doubt for reasons of
ergonomics every bit as much as of sound.
He was seen first of all with a Daphne Blue
made in 1967 (with a large headstock and
transition logo): his first electric guitar, chosen
initially because of its color, on which he
replaced the bridge pickup with a P90,
seeking a sound with greater body. This
beauty was very much in evidence on
the album sleeve of *Bop Till You Drop*,
released in 1979.

The modifications didn't stop there,
however, and in 1987, the first version of what

was to become known as the Coodercaster
appeared.

It was a sunburst Strat with a large
headstock, on which the neck pickup had
been replaced with a humbucker and the two
middle and bridge pickups had been removed
to allow room for an enormous Valco lap
steel pickup. The Valco company made
affordable instruments in Chicago in the
1950s and 1960s, and their lap steels
produced a particularly soft and transparent
sound. Some years later, the neck pickup was
to become a Teisco gold foil, thinner and
shinier than a humbucker. These particularly
pervasive adjustments were the recipe for
the Cooder sound, a recipe that worked so
well when it came to playing slide
that numerous enthusiastic amateurs and
boutique manufacturers came up with their
own version of the Coodercaster.

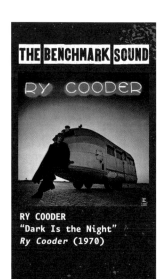

THE BENCHMARK SOUND

RY COODER

RY COODER
"Dark Is the Night"
Ry Cooder (1970)

Ry Cooder in 1994 ▶
for the New Orleans Jazzfest.

BURST
Duane Allman
THE SOUTHERN BURST

THE GENiUS OF SOUTHERN ROCK, DUANE ALLMAN, DiED iN 1971 AT THE AGE OF JUST 24. HE HAD RECORDED MUSiC WiTH ERiC CLAPTON, WiLSON PiCKETT, AND HiS OWN BAND, The Allman Brothers Band, using a superb collection of instruments along the way. Among the hand-picked group of guitars that he played, three Les Paul models stood out: a Goldtop from 1957 and two Bursts from 1959.

The first was his main guitar for the early days of the Allman Brothers, and the one that can be heard on Clapton's "Layla." In September 1970, the Allmans played a concert at Daytona Beach, and the band's first guitarist was playing a Les Paul, a superb Standard Cherry. Duane fell in love with this guitar, and offered to exchange it for his Goldtop, a Marshall amp, and $200 in cash (a not inconsiderable sum in those days). The deal went ahead, but before it did, Duane switched the pickups on the two guitars: he adored the look and playing feel of the 1959 but preferred the pickups from the 1957, and was therefore trying to get the best of both worlds. This Burst went on to become the most-recorded guitar in Allman's career, and it can be heard on the legendary live album made at Fillmore East in 1971.

In the middle of 1971, Duane was introduced to a guitar seller by Billy Gibbons from ZZ Top, who was already one of his customers, and bought another Burst from him, a more somber model whose headstock had already been broken and repaired. This Les Paul, later dubbed Hot 'Lanta, is the one that can be

seen in the photos from the final two months of the musician's life.

The two Les Paul Bursts were lovingly preserved and are now on display at the Rock 'n' Roll Hall of Fame in Cleveland, while the Goldtop can be found at the Big House Museum in Macon, Georgia. In 2014, the Allman Brothers played their farewell concert after forty-five years of good and loyal service, and the three guitars all made appearances in the hands of Warren Haynes and Derek Trucks, in an auditory tribute worthy of Duane.

◀ *Duane Allman in 1969 with the Goldtop that he played with a slide.*

MOSRITE
JOHNNY RAMONE

HEY HO LET'S GO

NO BAND CAN BE SAID TO REPRESENT THE AMERICAN VERSION OF PUNK BETTER THAN THE RAMONES. WITH THEIR DISTINCTIVE LOOK, ZOMBIES IN LEATHER JACKETS, they defined what was to be a simple, short, and diabolically effective onslaught of sound. None of their songs is more than two minutes long but many of them became classics, rallying cries, and sometimes even symbols that transcended music (how many teenagers wearing Ramones T-shirts have listened to one of the band's albums in full?) The equipment used by the band was perfectly in line with this image: cheap, sturdy stuff that could get bruised and battered without any need for special care. Johnny Ramone, the quartet's guitarist, is known above all for his association with the Mosrite Ventures II. Being a junkie, he had other financial priorities than guitars, and he therefore contented himself with the cheapest model he could find. The welcome bonus of the Mosrite is that it doesn't look like any other guitar. This signature model for the Ventures was the cheapest guitar in the Mosrite catalog in the 1960s, but its single-coil pickup was a little bit too weak to make Johnny's Marshall stacks roar, so he always replaced the bridge pickup (the only one he really used) with a DiMarzio Super Distortion, the ultimate workhorse humbucker. He appeared with several other instruments, but the Mosrite was to remain a constant from the Ramones' early days in 1974 right up to their split in 1996.

▲

Johnny Ramone in 1992 during a concert by The Ramones at the Hollywood Paladium.

PARKER
JONI MITCHELL
THE UNPREDICTABLE ONE

JONI MITCHELL IS A TRUE ORIGINAL. EVER SINCE SHE FIRST EMERGED ON CALIFORNIA'S FOLK SCENE IN THE LATE 1960S, SHE HAS NEVER STOPPED REINVENTING HERSELF AND CONQUERING the public and her peers through her resolutely non-conformist approach. None of her songs has been written in standard tuning, and Joni meanders with ease from one kind of tuning to another, depending on the needs of the song. In the early days, the only guitar she played was a Martin D-28, which consequently underwent all the different tunings used for the first five albums.

At the end of the 1970s, Mitchell switched to an electric guitar, opting for an Ibanez George Benson, and so as to avoid having to tune it on stage between every song, she had five identical guitars so that she could switch from one to the next.

But the real revolution arrived in 1995, when she was given a Roland VG-88. This multi-effects guitar system can receive the signal from a hexaphonic sensor that modifies the sound of each string independently from the five others. In other words, the guitar (in this case a luthier-made Strat, then a Parker Fly chosen because it was very comfortable and no doubt also because it was something unexpected) stays in standard tuning, but the VG-88 changes the tunings heard. Modern technology at the service of acoustic songs: you could say it's the best of both worlds.

◀ *Joni Mitchell on stage in 1996.*

JayDee
Tony Iommi
GUITAR-MAKING AT THE SERVICE OF THE DARK ARTS

◀ *The Epiphone SG Custom Tony Iommi - the version for left-handers, naturally.*

TONY IOMMI SINGLE-HANDEDLY WROTE THE RULEBOOK FOR HEAVY METAL AND COMPOSED ITS HEAVIEST, darkest, and most effective riffs. At the heart of Black Sabbath, his influence has made itself felt on every exponent of heavy metal, right up until today. The instruments he plays, designed for a left-hander with two fingertips missing, are as unusual as his approach to playing. In the band's early days, he fell in love with the Gibson SG, a model whose symmetrical shape means that it can easily be turned over and played by a left-hander, and whose devil's horns are highly appropriate for the dark lyrics of singer Ozzy Osbourne. In order to keep on playing without feeling any pain despite having lost two fingertips and replaced them with hardened leather caps, Iommi used ultra-lightweight strings tuned lower than normal, resulting in a slightly discordant effect whenever he attacked the guitar with venom. This accident only made the sound grow even bigger, and a large number of guitarists whose fingers were all present and correct went on to emulate this little trick.

After spending years on a Gibson modified by the luthier John Birch, and faced with the declining quality of the manufacturer's guitars, he asked Birch to make him an SG, and finally found what he wanted with a twenty-four-fret SG made by Jaydee, another small-scale guitar-making workshop. To date he has accumulated three signature models made by Gibson, Epiphone, and Jaydee, a testament to his significance as a musician.

STRATOCASTER
RITCHIE BLACKMORE
THE STRAT AT ITS HEAVIEST

IF ONLY... IF ONLY THERE WERE SOME SORT OF TECHNICAL CHARACTERISTIC THAT EXPLAINED IN SIMPLE TERMS THE ENORMOUS SOUND OF RITCHIE BLACKMORE and allowed the rest of us mere mortals to get anywhere near the incredible texture of "Space Truckin'" or "Woman From Tokyo"... And yet, in both Deep Purple and Rainbow, Blackmore stuck to a Strat, a guitar whose attack is very familiar but whose rich depth, in Blackmore's hands, is unrivalled. There was nothing romantic about his Strats: they were their master's tools, tools whose destiny was to be destroyed in moments of irritation (reputed to be very common for Ritchie), instruments bought new with no modifications, with a rosewood or maple fingerboard and a finish that might be black, white, or in three-tone sunburst.

The sole modification finally took place in 1973, the year in which Blackmore started scalloping his Strats — that is, scooping out the wood of the fingerboard between the frets so that he didn't need to apply as much pressure and could therefore do some spectacular bends without little effort. This still doesn't explain that sound of his, though... Part of the answer can be found in the arms race in his use of amps: his Marshall Major amp had 200 watts of power to start with, and was modified so that it could provide 278 watts (making it "the loudest amp in the world" at the time), and he boosted its input even more with a treble booster and the preamp of its reverb. Not so much in the background as at the foundations!

The Strat made by the Fender Custom Shop, inspired by Blackmore's black original.
▼

OLD BLACK
NEIL YOUNG
THE CRAFTSMAN AND HIS TOOL

WITH HIS LAID-BACK ATTITUDE AND GIVEN THE TRANCE-LIKE STATE TO WHICH HE SURRENDERS ON STAGE, ONE MIGHT WELL IMAGINE THAT NEIL YOUNG OPERATES ON FAR TOO LOFTY A PLANE TO CARE ABOUT TECHNICAL AND MATERIAL CONSIDERATIONS. In fact, he is a true obsessive. His official technician, Larry Cragg, will tell anyone who will listen that he's never had a client as demanding and punctilious as the Canadian genius. The amp he loves most is a Fender Deluxe from 1959, a time when this small 12-watt model was covered with tweed, and he's never played any concerts or made any recordings without this trusty companion by his side. Legend even has it that Young can tell just by listening the precise voltage that is delivered by an output, based on this amp's response.

When it comes to guitars, the man they call the Loner is a big collector, but there are two instruments in particular that he constantly comes back to. The Gretsch White Falcon from 1961 is a guitar with a body very similar to that of Chet Atkins's 6120, but with an even more sumptuous and 'blingy' decoration; Young's specific model is one of a very small number of stereo White Falcons: the three bass strings come out on one side, and the three treble strings on the other, so that each side can be connected to a different amp. This effect can be heard on the experimental album *Le Noise*. But Neil's final guitar, from which he is never separated, is a Gibson Les Paul nicknamed "Old Black." Old

Black began its life in 1953, and, like all the Les Pauls from that era, it had a beautiful goldtop finish, a very austere wraparound bridge, and two P90 pickups. When the guitar came into Young's possession, it had already been repainted black (somewhat amateurishly) and the bridge had been replaced with a Bigsby vibrato arm, a design that doesn't maintain the tuning particularly well but that Young is fond of due to the soft finesse of its action. Young completed the transformation by replacing the bridge pickup with a mini-humbucker gleaned from a Firebird (for greater bite than the original P90) and decorating it with a metallic pickguard, which no doubt also plays a role in the particularly mischievous personality of this Les Paul. Had these modifications been carried out by any other guitarist, they would have ruined the guitar's collectability, but Old Black has now become a legendary instrument, a relic in which part of Neil's inimitable sound lies hidden.

NEXT DOUBLE-PAGE SPREAD
With Crazy Horse in 1976 in London (Billy Talbot on bass, Frank Sampedro on second guitar).

THE BENCHMARK SOUND

NEIL YOUNG with CRAZY HORSE
EVERYBODY KNOWS THIS IS NOWHERE

NEIL YOUNG "Down By the River"
Everybody Knows This Is Nowhere (1969)

THE ACOUSTIC SIDE

Neil Young is one of that rare breed of guitarists who display the same level of talent on the acoustic guitar and the electric guitar, with a very personal playing style in both cases. Being a good Canadian lumberjack, he has a clear preference for Martin dreadnoughts, with a superb D-45 (the firm's most decorated and high-end model) from 1968 that can be heard on the album *Harvest*, and that is very much on view on the cover of his *Greatest Hits*. His main acoustic guitar today is a D-28 with a particularly rich history, as it previously belonged to Hank Williams, then Bob Dylan. The emotional weight attached to a guitar is the decisive factor for Young, who even wrote "This Old Guitar" about the Martin in question. For all that, he isn't put off by novelty, and was one of the first ambassadors of the manufacturer Taylor, to whom he gave tremendous visibility by playing his twelve-string model in the film he made in 1979, *Rust Never Sleeps*.

◄ Neil Young in the early 1970s playing a hybrid Martin, with a headstock from a D-45 and the body of a D-28.

117

STRATOCASTER
RORY GALLAGHER
IRELAND'S FINEST

◀ *Rory Gallagher on stage accompanied by his trusty Stratocaster.*

WHEN JIMI HENDRIX WAS ASKED WHAT IT FELT LIKE TO BE THE GREATEST GUITARIST IN THE WORLD, HIS REPLY WAS: "I DON'T KNOW, ASK RORY GALLAGHER." And one can only conclude that he was right, such was the brilliant Irishman's ability to develop an aural vocabulary and sound all of his own. Each of his concerts was a genuine tour de force during which he would take his pieces to a level far higher than the studio versions, thanks to his huge talent as an improviser. His choice of guitar was simple: he needed an instrument sturdy enough to deal with the rigors of the road (Gallagher was always on tour) but with a range big enough to keep up with his inspiration. The idea of the Strat therefore came to him quite naturally.

But not just any old Strat: it was the first ever Strat to arrive in Ireland, a 1961 model bought second-hand from a store in Cork. From 1963 onwards, he took it with him from one concert to the next and sweated all over it without restraint. His acidic sweat corroded the pickups, which had to be changed; it

corroded the neck, which became swollen and had to be taken off the guitar for six months to dry out; it distorted the pickguard, which was consequently replaced by another; and above all it corroded the lacquer, making the bare alder clearly visible between the few islands of sunburst that remained. This single object, Rory Gallagher's Strat, perfectly summarizes the romanticism of an instrument that displays the battle-scars received night after night, a romanticism that is only heightened by the fact that this Strat was used for all his concerts from 1963 right through to his death in 1995.

RED SPECIAL
BRIAN MAY
FROM A FIREPLACE TO WEMBLEY

FEW STORIES ILLUSTRATE THE PROVERB "NECESSITY IS THE MOTHER OF INVENTION" QUITE SO WELL AS THE CREATION OF THE RED SPECIAL.

Brian Harold May was 15 years old and wanted a guitar, like most British teenagers in 1963. His father was a skilled handyman, and the two of them therefore spent two years designing the instrument that Brian had pictured in his mind. The wood used for the body came from a table, the wood for the neck came from an old fireplace, the fingerboard inlays were made of mother-of-pearl buttons, and the vibrato arm was originally part of a bicycle saddlebag. In short, every element of the guitar was something that had been salvaged from odds and ends, with the exception of the three pickups, made by Burns and bought from a shop — though even these were modified. The whole thing was designed to suit the sound that May had dreamed up, from the hollow body designed to obtain lovely musical feedback, to the twenty-four-fret neck (a rarity at the time) with a very short scale, making it easy to hit the really high notes and bend the strings. The story might well have ended there and remained nothing more than a charming bit of romanticism. Except that after two years of taking the trouble not to leave out a single stage of the process, Brian managed to turn the Red Special (as he called his bit of gear) into a guitar that suited him perfectly. It could have been just a quirky and fun first guitar on which he could learn his trade before moving on to a proper guitar by a recognized maker, but his own musical voice and virtuosic playing style had developed in harmony with this gorgeous red number. It therefore remained his go-to guitar throughout his entire career at the heart of Queen, accompanying him wherever he went, from clubs to packed stadiums (including the gigantic Wembley Stadium) via the studios where it made itself heard on albums that have sold over 300 million copies.

A number of luthiers have made copies of the Red Special, but the original still can't be beaten, forty years after its creation. It was quite an amazing outcome for an instrument cobbled together out of part of a table and part of a fireplace.

THE BENCHMARK SOUND

QUEEN "Killer Queen"
Sheer Heart Attack
(1974)

*Brian May during ▶
a concert in the
Netherlands in 1979.*

**NEXT DOUBLE-
PAGE SPREAD**
*Alongside Freddie
Mercury in 1978.*

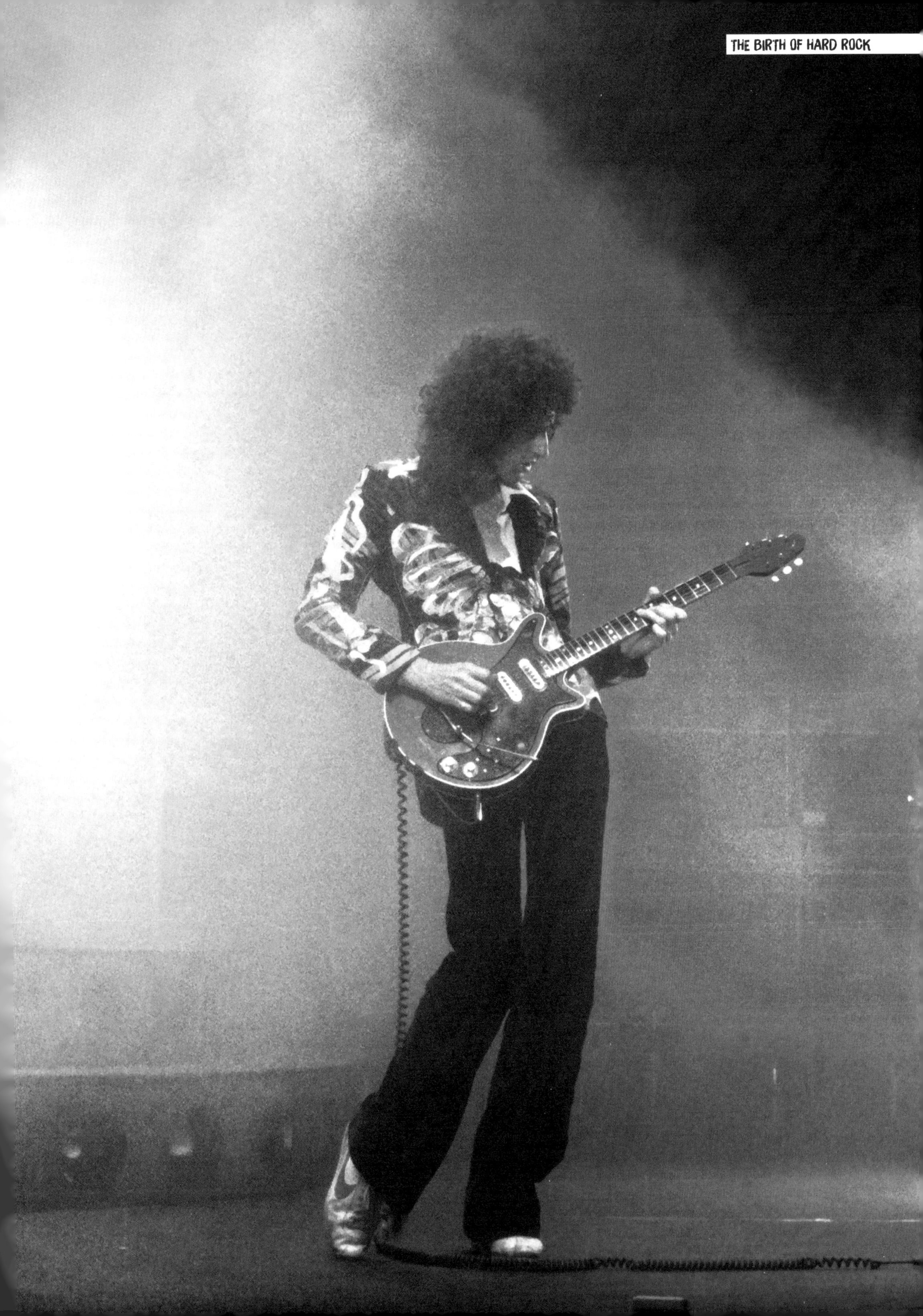

5 INDISPENSABLE HARD ROCK ALBUMS

AS THE 1970S LOOMED ON THE HORIZON, BRITISH BANDS BEGAN TO GET ANGRY, THEIR AMPS BECAME MORE POWERFUL, THEIR SINGERS SOARED TO NEW HEIGHTS, AND THEIR GUITARISTS TURNED THEMSELVES INTO VIRTUOSOS. SLOWLY BUT SURELY, HARD ROCK WAS BEING BORN, AND THIS TRANSITION PERIOD GAVE US SOME EXTREMELY EXCITING ALBUMS. HERE ARE FIVE ALBUMS RELEASED BETWEEN 1969 AND 1972 THAT DEFINED THE STYLE.

LED ZEPPELIN, ▶
LED ZEPPELIN II (1969)
Led Zeppelin's first album still seems to waver between blues and folk, but this second opus, released a few months later, leaves no room whatsoever for ambiguity. The sonic worlds they create remain very diverse, but the sound of the Les Paul is huge and the riffs are obscenely juicy, from the opening of "Whole Lotta Love" to "Heartbreaker" and its solo lying at the edge of the precipice, to the ending to "Bring It On Home."

BLACK SABBATH, ▶
PARANOID (1970)
There were already a few very heavy riffs on the first, eponymous album by the band from Birmingham, but it was in this album that they really stepped into the light as specialists in the nascent genre of heavy metal. The tracks "Paranoid" and "War Pigs" soon became anthems, but in terms of heavy, viscous, and utterly unwholesome ambience, nothing compares with "Electric Funeral."

MOUNTAIN, *CLIMBING!* (1970) ▶

Mountain are the only American rock band in this selection, and their first album is a classic that remains unsurpassed in many respects. The band plays with a feverish energy, the compositions are excellent, and the playing of the lead guitarist Leslie West is brutal, intense, and melodious in equal measure. From the hit "Mississippi Queen" and its memorable riff to the melancholic sound of "Theme for an Imaginary Western," there is plenty to appreciate.

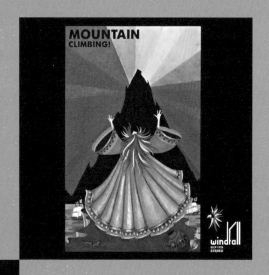

◀ HUMBLE PIE, *PERFORMANCE ROCKIN' THE FILLMORE* (1971)

Recorded over the course of four concerts at the legendary American concert venue Fillmore East, this live album is a wonderful demonstration of power and mastery. The soloist Peter Frampton is present for the final round, and he plays in it as never before, combining blues roots and jazz inflections with great finesse. The impeccably rhythmical playing and the fiendish voice of Steve Marriott complete a superb tableau.

DEEP PURPLE, ▶ MACHINE HEAD (1972)

Machine Head was the band's sixth album, no less, but if the world were only able to keep one for posterity, it would no doubt be this one. In it, the band finds the style that was to remain theirs until the present day, and the compositions are Deep Purple's finest of all time. The album is known, of course, for the timeless "Smoke On The Water," a cause of injured fingers for many a beginner, but the tracks "Highway Star," "Lazy," and "Pictures Of Home" stand out as the most exciting musical journeys.

GIBSON BYRDLAND
TED NUGENT
THE JAZZ BOX THAT PLAYED ROCK MUSIC

PASSIONS ALWAYS RUN HIGH WHEN TED NUGENT IS MENTIONED, UNFORTUNATELY MORE IN CONNECTION WITH HIS POLITICAL PHILOSOPHY THAN WITH HIS MUSIC.

Indeed, the musician known as the "motor city madman" is a huge gun enthusiast, hunts stags for their meat, and advocates survivalism.

Beneath this frankly oafish and Neanderthal exterior, however, his choices of guitars reveal all his inner subtlety and finesse.

Whereas you would naturally expect his macho hard rock to be played on a Les Paul or an SG, he chose another landmark guitar by Gibson that had absolutely nothing to do with these: the Byrdland.

Released in 1955, this was a double signature model, since it was born out of the joint vision of guitarists Billy Byrd and Hank Garland. It is a chunky guitar intended for jazz, whose spruce top and maple body are reminiscent of a version of the L-5 with a shallower body and a shorter neck. The Byrdland was thus designed to be used as part of a light sound, not for the obscene volume at which Nugent plays, a volume at which the guitar is very soon overcome by uncontrollable feedback. But Ted is a cowboy and he rode the feedback in the same way you would tame a bucking mustang. He systematically sought out the part of the stage that would allow him to get a musical, satisfying feedback, and was forever tinkering with his volume and tone knobs so as to control the feedback when it came. Due to this handling and his acidic sweat, the lacquer gave way to bare wood on his most-used guitars, and this perspiration forced his technician to replace the pickups that couldn't withstand it.

Today, Ted Nugent has a collection of seventeen Byrdland guitars, all of which have been branded with a hot iron with the initials TN and with a number, so that he can keep track of his flock.

> "IT'S NOT ABOUT MANAGING IT, IT'S ABOUT SUCCUMBING TO IT."

Ted Nugent on stage in London in 1979. ▶

128

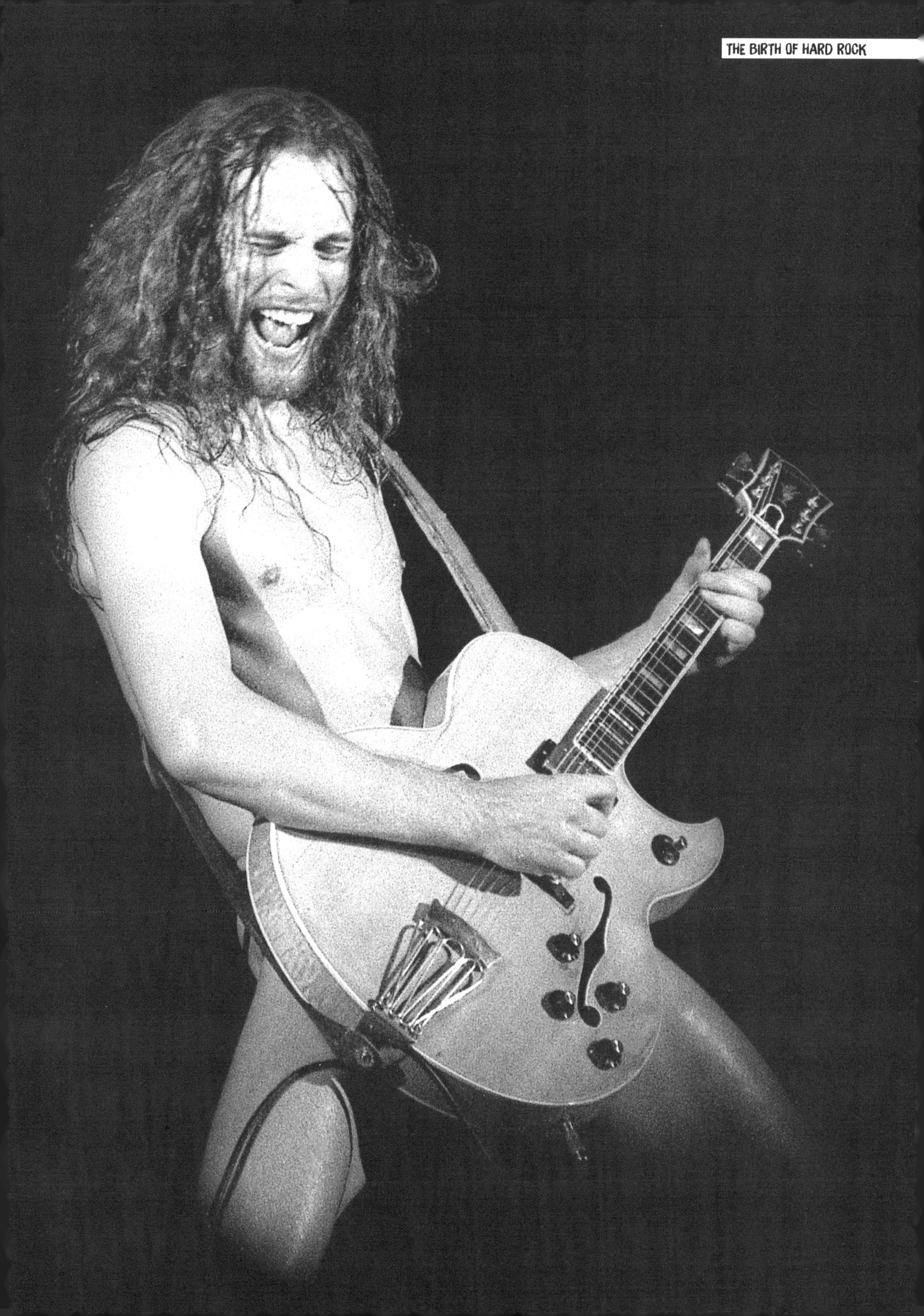

LES PAUL CUSTOM
PETER FRAMPTON

THE REVENANT

THE BRITISH BLUES ROCK OUTFIT HUMBLE PIE WAS PLAYING AT FILLMORE WEST, THE LEGENDARY CONCERT VENUE IN SAN FRANCISCO. Their flamboyant soloist, Peter Frampton, who turned 20 that year, 1970, was looking for a guitar to replace his ES-335, whose semi-hollow body was creating major problems with feedback, given the deafening volume at which the band played its raging music. It was then that a friend of his suggested that Frampton try his guitar, a Gibson Les Paul Custom made in 1954 and heavily modified to convert it to the specifications from 1957, replacing the two original single-coil pickups with three humbuckers and enlarging the cavities in the wood in the process.

Naturally, Frampton fell under this beauty's spell, and his friend decided to make a gift of the guitar to him. From that moment on, it accompanied the virtuoso for the next ten years of his career, and so its neck can be seen on the cover of the double live album *Frampton Comes Alive!*, the biggest-selling album of 1976.

In 1980, the plane carrying all the equipment for his tour of South America crashed in Panama; all the instruments were devoured by the flames, and Peter was left mourning the loss of the great beauty. In the 1990s, Gibson made a reproduction of the original for him, and it went on to become one of the best-sellers among the firm's signature models.

In 2010, a guitarist from Curaçao took his guitar along to an amateur luthier, who recognized it and made sure that word got to Frampton: the Les Paul hadn't been destroyed by the fire after all, it had been saved from the wreckage. Two years later, the guitarist finally agreed to sell his instrument, and the Custom, which was naturally given the nickname Phoenix, was reunited with its former owner and began touring again as if the two had never been apart.

◀ *Frampton and his Les Paul Custom in 1976, the year of* Frampton Comes Alive!

THE BENCHMARK SOUND

Frampton Comes Alive!

PETER FRAMPTON
" Do You Feel Like We Do "
Frampton Comes Alive!
(1976)

131

AC/DC
LET THERE BE GUITAR

FOR A BAND WHOSE CAREER SPANNED FORTY-THREE YEARS AND WHICH HAD TWO GUITARISTS (Angus Young on lead and Malcolm Young, recently replaced by his cousin Stevie Young, on rhythm), the cast-list of instruments that have appeared on stage with these raging Australians is far from enormous. The Malcolm side of things is the most straightforward, because, with the exception of a Gretsch White Falcon briefly used during the *Back in Black* (1980) period, which obscured him from view almost completely due to his diminutive size, the elder of the two brothers stayed loyal to a single guitar throughout his entire career.

This guitar, a Gretsch Jet Firebird made in 1963, was given to him by his brother George Young, himself a guitarist of the successful band The Easybeats. It had already been modified by the addition of a third, middle pickup, but Malcolm quickly adapted the instrument to his own extremely simplistic philosophy: it was goodbye to the two middle and neck pickups, goodbye to the red color as well, goodbye to the switches and knobs that no longer served a purpose, and goodbye to the original tuning machines. What was left was a natural Gretsch on which the wood was visible, and whose solitary bridge pickup was sufficient to produce the super-charged growl that Malcolm was looking for. Of course, the enormous 12-58 strings had a

role in that too. Gretsch released a signature model in the 1990s, but its new look seemed bizarre to anyone who was familiar with the original version. The original was therefore recreated right down to the tiniest details by the manufacturer's Custom Shop in 2017. As far as Angus Young is concerned, the Gibson SG, with its light and refined shape, perfect for a man of his size and for his frenzied playing style, is indispensable. He never appeared in his band with any other model, but nonetheless got through several dozen of them that did not necessarily stand up to his unbridled energy and to AC/DC's touring pace. The electronics had to be changed regularly due to the sweat that wreaked havoc on the components, despite efforts to protect their cavities using scotch tape.

The SG with which he is most often associated, and the one that served as the basis for his first signature Gibson, is a red model made in 1970 with a large pickguard and the Lyre Vibrola vibrato arm. His second signature model was black and had no vibrato arm. Like Tony Iommi, he too had an SG built for him by the Jaydee workshop, but seemed to prefer the 1960s Gibson that he still tours with today.

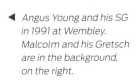

◀ *Angus Young and his SG in 1991 at Wembley. Malcolm and his Gretsch are in the background, on the right.*

AC/DC
"Stiff Upper Lip"
Stiff Upper Lip (2000)

HIGH FREQUENCIES

Sometimes, a simple, seemingly trivial detail can change everything. A fan of the band with a discerning ear was trying to recreate Angus Young's sound right down to the smallest details. He therefore procured an SG of the same vintage and a Marshall Plexi (the 50-watt version of the 1959 model, preferred to the 100-watt version due to its ability to provide earlier distortion), to no avail, because Young had never played with a pedal at his feet. Despite that, and in spite of an impressive ability to reproduce his idol's use of vibrato and his touch, the sound continued to escape him. But then he had a revelation, while re-reading an old interview for a specialist magazine in which Angus himself provided the answer by explaining that he also used his high-frequency wireless system in the studio. So the little box wasn't just used so that he could move around the stage easily: it provided a degree of compression that pleased the guitarist's ear. The fan tracked down a Schaffer-Vega Diversity System from that time period, and sure enough, the sound he had coveted for so long finally came pouring forth from his amp.

Angus Young on the ▶
shoulders of Bon Scott, the
band's first singer, in 1977.

LES PAUL JUNIOR
LESLIE WEST
NOT JUST FOR BEGINNERS

IN 1954, GIBSON RELEASED TWO VERSIONS OF THE LES PAUL, SEEKING TO ATTRACT BOTH THE MOST WELL-OFF MUSICIANS (THE LES PAUL CUSTOM) AND THOSE WHO WERE JUST STARTING OUT.

The Les Paul Junior is extremely simple, with a mahogany body with no maple top, a wraparound bridge, a solitary P90 pickup, and no decoration at all. As a result of this simplicity and its very affordable price, there was a time when the Junior could be acquired for just a few bucks in any pawnshop in America.

In 1967, the bassist Felix Pappalardi produced the album *Disraeli Gears* for Cream and became friends with Eric Clapton. He went in search of a guitar that Clapton had left in a store in New York to be repaired. The store had lost it, and the manager offered him a Junior by way of recompense. The guitarist Leslie West was with him at the time, and he was impressed by the incendiary level of output from the little P90. From that moment forth he made the Junior his go-to guitar, a contrarian solution that created an eye-catching contrast with the guitarist's larger-than-life frame. On witnessing the success enjoyed by Mountain, West and Pappalardi's band, true connoisseurs like Keith Richards or Mick Ralphs (Mott the Hoople) began to take an interest in the Junior, a model that has now reached vertiginous heights.

▲
Leslie West in 2007 with his signature model Dean, a direct descendant of his original Les Paul Junior.

THE BENCHMARK SOUND

MOUNTAIN
"Mississippi Queen"
Climbing (1970)

JOAN JETT
"Bad Reputation"
Bad Reputation (1980)

THE BENCHMARK SOUND

MELODY MAKER
JOAN JETT

NOT JUST FOR CHILDREN

BEFORE BECOMING THE SOLO STAR SHE'S KNOWN AS TODAY, JOAN JETT PLAYED RHYTHM GUITAR IN THE RUNAWAYS, A HARD ROCK BAND FROM THE LATE 1970S, known to the general public as the first band made up solely of women to achieve hits in this genre of music. At the time, Jett played a Les Paul that was far too heavy and that she found uncomfortable. Furthermore, she only used the bridge pickup, and so she was looking for a simpler instrument, which would give her more freedom to move around on stage without the impediment of an 11-pound guitar around her neck.

It was then that she was introduced to the Melody Maker. This model by Gibson was launched in 1959, when the maker realized that the Les Paul Junior was prohibitively expensive for many beginners. They therefore designed a guitar that was even simpler, with a slimmer body and a smaller neck, which garnered a reputation as the perfect instrument for children who were starting to learn to play (it was Billy Gibbons' first guitar, for example). The idea of subverting the Melody Maker's original function was perfectly in line with Jett's punk philosophy, and she adopted it straight away. She replaced the single-coil pickups, with their very clacking sound, with fatter humbuckers, then ultimately took off the neck pickup. Forty years on, the white beauty is still her main guitar.

▲
Joan Jett on stage in the early 1980s.

137

ESQUIRE
BRUCE SPRINGSTEEN
THE BOSS'S WIFE

◄ *Bruce Springsteen and his trusty steed in 1984.*

BRUCE SPRINGSTEEN IS MORE THAN A GUITARIST, HE'S A SYMBOL. HE'S THE FAVORITE SINGER OF THE LITTLE MAN, THE FORGOTTEN AND OVERLOOKED RESIDENTS OF THE AMERICAN HEARTLAND, AND THE BELEAGUERED MANUAL LABORERS WHO ARE ALWAYS down on their luck. Concerts by the man they call The Boss are veritable religious experiences that last upwards of three hours, during which the guitar becomes both totem pole and antenna. As the hard grafter he is, Springsteen owed it to himself to have a simple, reliable instrument capable of lasting the distance in his epic concerts with the E Street Band.

In the early 1970s, Bruce played a Les Paul, an instrument that was far too sophisticated and sensitive for his style of playing. And so it came about that in 1973, he met the one who was to become his inseparable companion for decades to come. In perfect harmony with the singer's chiseled looks, the guitar was assembled from two different instruments, and it had a life that was as turbulent as they come before ending up in the arms of The Boss. The neck came from a 1957 Esquire — the simplistic guitar *par excellence* — while the body was that of a 1950s Telecaster, heavily modified. In the 1960s, session musicians would sometimes resort to rather crooked practices in order to get paid as much as possible, and in the rules drawn up by their union it was specified that a musician could earn wages on each different part that he played.

The Telecaster in question had therefore been fitted with four pickups with four independent outputs in order to record on four channel strips at once and thereby produce four paid parts in a single take.

This components used in this electronic scam had been removed when Bruce bought the guitar, but what remained was a body that was more hollow than normal, and was therefore even lighter than that of a normal Tele, a considerable benefit when you're playing for three hours every night. As the ultimate symbol of the way this guitar was played without any restraint, it had to be covered with a waterproof lacquer to protect it from the gallons of sweat that cascaded down over it.

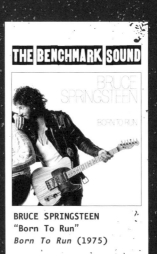

THE BENCHMARK SOUND

BRUCE SPRINGSTEEN
"Born To Run"
Born To Run (1975)

FRANKENSTRAT

EDDIE VAN HALEN

THE ORIGINAL SUPERSTRAT

IN THE 1980S, LES PAULS AND TELECASTERS WERE COMPLETELY OUT OF FASHION.

Musicians would to sell them on for next to nothing in hopes of being able to progress to the most prized guitar of the day, the Superstrat, which was a Stratocaster modernized by means of "enhancements" such as a Floyd Rose vibrato arm and a humbucker pickup on the bridge (and sometimes on the neck). And who was to blame? A single individual was responsible for this revolution, and his famous "brown sound" continues to haunt the dreams of the greatest guitarists on the planet today. Eddie Van Halen, the founder of the band Van Halen, was a very influential inventor on the musical front (everyone wanted to imitate him by trying out tapping, though no one could do it as well as him, obviously), but he was also a DIY genius on the instrument. The original idea for the legendary guitar he planned to make was to design a hybrid that would sound like a Gibson but be as comfortable as a Fender. To achieve this blend, he started with a body and neck purchased at a knock-off price at the workshop of Wayne Charvel, a spare parts specialist at the time. He then called on two organ donors, a 1958 Stratocaster from which he retrieved the traditional Fender vibrato arm, and an ES-335 from 1960 whose bridge pickup was put in the bridge position on the maestro's new creation, not without having first been dipped in wax to make it more resistant to parasites. Eddie cut out the pickguard himself from a vinyl disc, shaping it so that it would hide the hole left by the absence of second and third pickups; he painted the body black, then white, using masking tape to cover certain areas so that he eventually achieved the striped effect that can be seen on the sleeve of his first, eponymous album from 1978.

The guitarist instantly became a superstar whom everyone tried to imitate, and, as such, numerous guitar manufacturers started coming up with their own version of the guitar. Anxious not to have the same guitar as every Tom, Dick, and Harry, Eddie continued to make alterations to his own, so that it ended up being dubbed the Frankenstrat. He added some red stripes to the finish, installed a Floyd Rose vibrato arm, the first relatively reliable model, which he kept in place with a quarter, and decorated the back with tail light reflectors from a truck, which really soaked up the light when he was on stage. Finally, with the aim of misleading all the copycats, he fitted a single-coil pickup in the neck position and a three-way selector switch: needless to say, none of this was actually connected.

Eddie Van Halen ▶
in an outfit designed to match his Frankenstrat, in the dressing room of a concert hall in 1981.

THE BENCHMARK SOUND

VAN HALEN "Eruption"
Van Halen (1978)

A MUSEUM PIECE

Eddie Van Halen had numerous other guitars over the course of his career, from the variations on the Frankenstrat designed in partnership with the makers who endorsed him, to the signature models more akin to a Les Paul in spirit, like the models he had made by Music Man, then by Peavey. The Frankenstrat remained a real fan favorite, though, doubtless because it was the one he was playing when his first album came out, the album through which the whole world discovered him, but also because it symbolized the entrepreneurial spirit that is so dear to the hearts of Americans, that Californian myth of the spare-time craftsman tinkering away in his garage and eventually emerging with a tool ready to create a revolution. In 2007, Eddie teamed up with Fender to offer a very limited edition series of replicas, and the Custom Shop went to extremely painstaking lengths in its efforts to produce a credible replica, including getting hold of 1971 quarters! One of these replicas can now be seen at the National Museum of American History in Washington, D.C.

Eddie Van Halen on stage ▶
in 1984, holding another
version of the Frankenstrat.

STRATOCASTER
STEVIE RAY VAUGHAN
THE TEXAN

Stevie Ray Vaughan's original Stratocaster, Number One.
▼

HOW MANY GUITARISTS DO YOU NEED TO PLAY STEVIE RAY VAUGHAN? ALL OF THEM, APPARENTLY! This classic joke reveals a lot about a widespread adoration, an unusual consensus in this rough and tough world. What's more, one of the few other guitarists to have created this kind of unanimity was the man who influenced SRV more than anyone else, Jimi Hendrix. Stevie brought the blues back into fashion as an antidote to the plastic pop of the 1980s, proving that style still had a *raison d'être* in the age of synthesizers. It has been said that the huge sound he extracted from his Strat had something about it that elicited yearning, with that very specific mixture of depth and snappy attack.

Among the plethora of Fenders that passed through his hands, two Strats clearly stood out as favorites. The first, known simply as Number One, was his main guitar from 1973 until his death in 1990. It was a model that brought together pickups from 1959, a neck from 1962, and a body made in 1963, suggesting that the guitar was an assembly job, even though it was a common practice at Fender to use pre-prepared components whose dates of manufacturing weren't necessarily very close together. The changes made by Stevie were essentially visual ones, with the white pickguard replaced with a pickguard adorned with his initials and the standard vibrato arm replaced with a gold left-handed vibrato arm, an obvious nod to Hendrix, the left-hander who played on right-handed models and so had his vibrato arm next to the bass strings. SRV was by no means gentle in his attack, as evidenced by the fact that more wood than lacquer can be seen on the body, and so he fitted some enormous strings to his Strat, 13-58s.

His next favorite guitar was Lenny, the re-finished Strat 63 given to him as a gift in 1980 by his wife Lenora, hence the nickname. The two guitars were painstakingly reproduced by the Fender Custom Shop and Lenny was sold at auction for the princely sum of $623,500, whereas Number One has never parted from the Vaughan family.

Stevie Ray Vaughan ▶
on stage in 1983 with his
famous guitar strap with
musical notes on it, almost as
famous as the guitar itself.

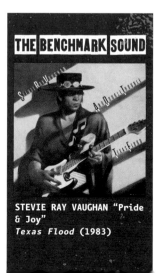

THE BENCHMARK SOUND

STEVIE RAY VAUGHAN "Pride & Joy"
Texas Flood (1983)

STRATOCASTER
NILE RODGERS
THE HITMAKER

▲
The Hitmaker reproduced down to the smallest details by the Fender Custom Shop.

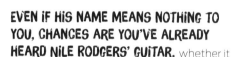

EVEN IF HIS NAME MEANS NOTHING TO YOU, CHANCES ARE YOU'VE ALREADY HEARD NILE RODGERS' GUITAR, whether it was at the heart of the funk band Chic or alongside one of the countless superstars who have called upon his talents as a producer, from David Bowie to Madonna via Diana Ross, Robert Plant, Michael Jackson, Mick Jagger, Jeff Beck, and Duran Duran. For younger readers, Rodgers is the man to whom we owe the driving rhythm of Daft Punk's smash hit "Get Lucky." Normally, when a musician plays with so many stars in such radically different styles, he or she does so with a whole arsenal of instruments, in order to adapt to each artist's musical world in the best possible way. Nile Rodgers, by contrast, has played the same instrument throughout his entire career, a hardtail (with no vibrato arm) Fender Stratocaster, dubbed The Hitmaker because it is estimated that his music has generated over two billion dollars' worth of album sales.

In 1973, Rodgers was playing a huge jazz-style Gibson, which didn't correspond in any way to the funky sound he wanted to get out of it. His bassist, Bernard Edwards, suggested that he move on to a Strat. They went to a pawnshop and chose the cheapest one they could find, whose low price was explained by its dubious originality. The body is from 1960, the neck is from 1959 (hence the maple fingerboard, which was no longer present on the models from 1960), the pickups are from 1969, and the pickguard is made of copper. To top the whole bizarre picture off, the Hitmaker has huge control knobs reminiscent of the ones on a Gibson, something that no doubt facilitated the transition for Nile Rodgers. In 2013, when the luthiers at the Fender Custom Shop were measuring every tiny detail with a view to creating a replica, they unanimously said that they had never seen a Strat like it, though they had been up close and personal with more Fenders than most guitarists will see in a lifetime. Sometimes, then, you just stumble upon the perfect combination without even having to look for it.

▲
Nile on stage at a festival in London's Hyde Park, ever faithful to his Strat Hitmaker, in 2015.

CHIC

chic cheer   i want your love
le freak   at last i am free
savoir faire sometimes you win
happy man   (funny) bone

**CHIC
"Le Freak"
C'est Chic (1978)**

STRATOCASTER MARK KNOPFLER
THE ECHO OF HANK

WHEN YOU THINK ABOUT IT, THERE'S SOMETHING INCREDIBLY MOVING ABOUT THE FACT THAT ROCK STARS HAVE IDOLS, TOO. Even the guitarists that we worship and whose equipment we painstakingly pick apart have also passionately studied the instruments of those who inspired them to play. Why do you think it was that Mark Knopfler, who founded the band Dire Straits in 1977, always played on red Fender Stratocasters, so much so that they became his trademark guitar? It was quite simply because Mark was a huge fan of the Shadows. For an admirer of Hank Marvin, the red Strat represented an ideal that could never be surpassed.

At the age of 19, when his band was preparing to release its first album, he procured his first serious guitar, the one against which all the later ones were to be judged: a 1961 Strat with a rosewood fingerboard whose paint had been sanded off so as to achieve the famous "natural wood" look that everyone was seeking in the 1970s. Knopfler hastened to repaint it in red, to give it the famous Fiesta Red hue he had been looking for since the beginning.

A few months later, when the band was making waves on the London scene, Mark bought a second red Strat, this time with a maple fingerboard. It was presented as a 1962, but at that time, Fender only made rosewood fingerboards. Some years later, when the luthier John Suhr disassembled it, he realized that the guitar was in fact an amalgamation of different parts, including appointments that came from a Japanese copy. Knopfler was so disappointed that he replaced it with a Schecter in 1980. At the time, the manufacturer was mainly making copies of Fenders, and the one that caught his eye was naturally a red Strat with a maple fingerboard. A leopard doesn't change its spots.

Mark Kopfler with ▶
Dire Straits on July 13, 1985,
during the epic fundraising
concert "Live Aid."

THE BENCHMARK SOUND

DIRE STRAITS

DIRE STRAITS
"Sultans Of Swing"
Dire Straits (1978)

EXPLORER
THE EDGE
WITH OR WITHOUT YOU

THE EDGE, THE SONIC ARCHITECT OF THE BAND U2, IS KNOWN ABOVE ALL FOR HIS ABSOLUTELY COLOSSAL ARSENAL OF EFFECTS, an electronic collage providing textures that have been endlessly copied by all the guitarists in modern-day pop. But whereas all of these copycats tend to play very traditional guitars like a Strat or a Les Paul, Dave Evans (aka The Edge) chose an instrument so original that it instantly became associated with him: the Gibson Explorer. This enormous guitar was released in 1958, at the same time as the Flying V, and was even more of an abject failure than the latter. The first re-editions came out in 1976, ten years after the first re-editions of the Flying V, and, in those days, news travelled very slowly in the world of guitars.

So it was that on that day in 1978, when the young Dave walked into a store in New York while on holiday with his parents, he knew nothing at all about the Explorer. What's more, he had wanted to buy a Les Paul, but he immediately fell in love with the bizarre creature he saw before him. On his return to Ireland, the rest of the band had their doubts, but they ended up being convinced by the sound it produced. And it was a good thing too, for when U2 later became the huge global pop machine that they are today, the Explorer used for every album and concert was to become The Edge's model, once and for all. Despite his attachment to this guitar, he sold the original at auction in 2008, with the proceeds going to the musicians of New Orleans affected by Hurricane Katrina. The very definition of class.

◀ *The Edge and his two indispensable props: his beanie and his Explorer.*

RICK TURNER
LINDSEY BUCKINGHAM
AN UNUSUAL GUITAR FOR AN UNUSUAL STYLE OF PLAYING

IF YOU LOOK CLOSELY AT A STRATOCASTER, YOU'LL NOTICE THAT THE BRIDGE PICKUP IS POSITIONED AT AN ANGLE SO THAT IT IS CLOSER TO THE NECK UNDERNEATH THE BASS STRINGS, on the very simple principle that the closer a pickup is to the bridge, the better it will be at capturing the string's higher and more aggressive frequencies. But why entrust such an important element of the sound to the manufacturer, when you could control it yourself? It was on the basis of this principle that Lindsey Buckingham, the guitarist and singer who brought new life to Fleetwood Mac in 1975, used the rotating pickup fitted on the guitar designed by the Californian luthier Rick Turner. The famous Model 1 replaced the Les Paul Custom that he was using before, and that gave him a classic rock look that didn't sit well either with the band's pop and progressive aspirations or with his own playing, an iconoclastic blend of acoustic fingerpicking and Hendrix-esque savagery.

To bring out the best in this hybrid aspect, the Turner is fitted with a piezoelectric sensor, which makes it possible to get an electro-acoustic sound out of a solid body guitar. Buckingham therefore plugged the guitar into two amp systems at the same time, and has been taking full advantage of the possibilities that this model opens up for nearly forty years.

Rick Turner Model 1.
▼

THE BENCHMARK SOUND

LINDSEY BUCKINGHAM "Don't Look Down"
Out Of the Cradle (1992)

5 PEDALS THAT CHANGED THE WORLD

IT'S DIFFICULT NOWADAYS TO FIND A GUITARIST WHO DOESN'T HAVE A PANOPLY OF PEDALS AT HIS OR HER FEET. AND YET THIS HASN'T ALWAYS BEEN THE CASE, SUCH HAS BEEN THE RELATIVELY SLOW PACE OF DEVELOPMENT IN THE FIELD OF EFFECTS. AS THIS EVOLUTION HAS GRADUALLY OCCURRED, SOME PEDALS HAVE BEEN TRUE PHENOMENA AS A RESULT OF BEING ASSOCIATED WITH LEGENDARY MOMENTS IN THE HISTORY OF ROCK. HERE ARE THE FIVE MOST FAMOUS PEDALS OF ALL.

◄ MAESTRO FUZZ-TONE Z-1 (1962)

The fuzz effect is a very rounded and woolly distortion that makes your guitar sound like a saxophone or a broken amp. Several pioneering players achieved it through bits of trickery (in some cases by actually breaking their amps), but the first pedal to capture this sound in a box was the Maestro Fuzz-Tone. It remains forever associated with the first fuzz riff that made the whole world prick up its ears, "(I Can't Get No) Satisfaction" by the Rolling Stones, in which Keith Richards uses it to imitate a brass part.

VOX WAH (1967) ►

The first musician to be endorsed by Vox, when they released this legendary pedal, was Clyde McCoy, a trumpeter, who used it to imitate the effect of a mute with his foot. The wah-wah shifts a peak from the mid-bass register towards the mid-treble, creating an approximate imitation of the human voice. This gliding effect can be found in the intro to Jimi Hendrix's "Voodoo Child (Slight Return)," in Isaac Hayes's "Shaft" and in most of the solos by Kirk Hammett (of Metallica).

MXR PHASE 90 (1974) ▶

The Phase 90 was the first pedal ever produced by MXR, and in producing it the company instigated a revolution, such is the extent to which it has become a veritable pedal empire. The Phase 90 is a pedal whose solitary knob controls the speed of the effect, a modulation that plays on the phase shift to create the impression that the sound is turning in a cyclical motion. The bandwagon effect was sweepingly widespread, and the MXR could be heard at the time on everything from country albums to funk and rock, right up to Johnny Winter, who made very frequent use of it.

◀ DIGITECH WHAMMY (1989)

This pedal is based on a very simple idea that instantly nudged awake the creative muse inside Tom Morello (of Rage Against the Machine) and Dimebag Darrell (Pantera): it shifts the note up an octave, or up two octaves, thereby creating a very high sound that takes the listener by surprise and makes dogs prick up their ears. More recently, Jack White has demonstrated that this pedal is also perfectly suited to garage rock of the most unbridled kind.

BOSS CE-1 ▶
CHORUS ENSEMBLE (1976)

Another pedal maker, another empire. The Japanese firm Roland enjoyed so much success with the chorus integrated into their Jazz Chorus series of amps that they decided to offer the effect in the form of a separate pedal. In order to attract guitarists more specifically, they created the brand Boss, which remains forever associated with dozens of colored pedals that every guitarist has used at some time or other. The rich and profound effect of the CE-1 can be heard in the music of Andy Summers (The Police), John Frusciante (Red Hot Chili Peppers), and Alex Lifeson (Rush).

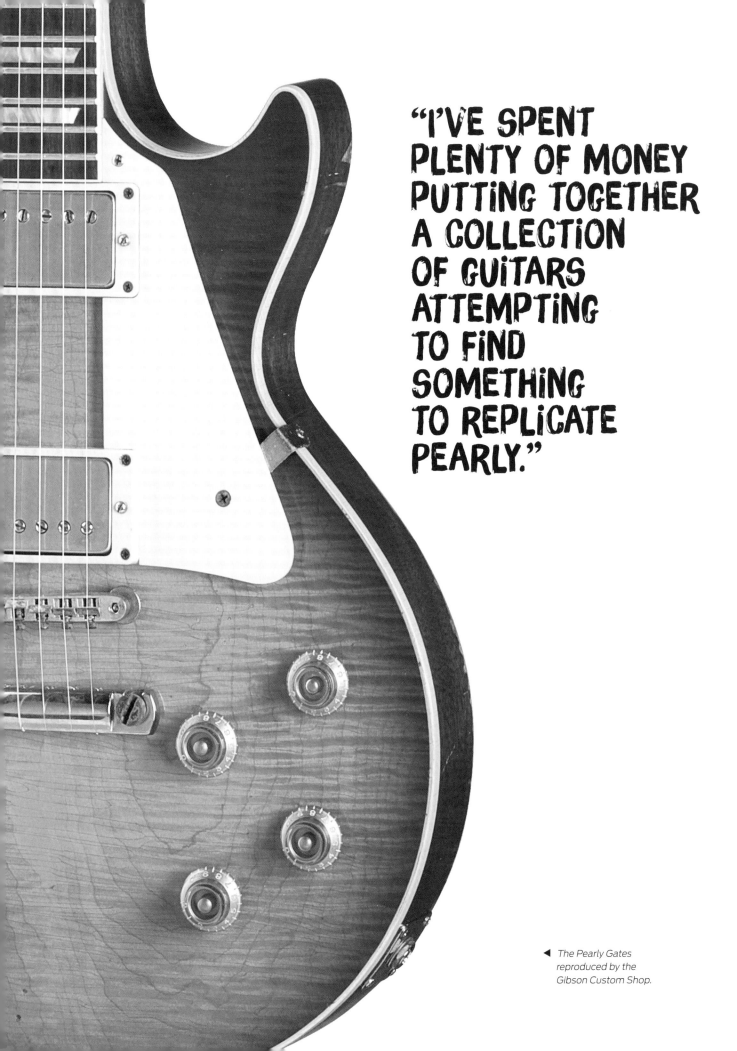

"I'VE SPENT PLENTY OF MONEY PUTTING TOGETHER A COLLECTION OF GUITARS ATTEMPTING TO FIND SOMETHING TO REPLICATE PEARLY."

◀ *The Pearly Gates reproduced by the Gibson Custom Shop.*

PEARLY GATES
BILLY GIBBONS
DESTINY

BILLY GIBBONS, WHO HAS BEEN LEADER OF THE TRIO ZZ TOP CONTINUOUSLY SINCE 1969, POSSESSES ONE OF THE MOST IMPRESSIVE GUITAR COLLECTIONS in the world, and while he has never revealed it, rumors abound that he has multiple hangars full of guitars, and that he doesn't miss a single year or a single color of all the models made by the big manufacturers, from the classic to the quirky. And yet, in this immodest arms race, one particular guitar has remained top of the tree ever since the start, to the point that it has become one of the best-known Bursts among the general public.

At the end of the 1960s, Gibbons lent a car to his actress friend so that she could travel from Texas to Hollywood for an audition. The car was in terrible shape, but it got her there, and she ended up getting the part. The valiant automobile was thus given the nickname "Pearly Gates." Once she had reached her destination, the actress sold the car and sent $250 to Gibbons as compensation.

Gibbons, blown away by John Mayall's album *Bluesbreakers With Eric Clapton*, was looking for a sunburst Les Paul Standard, and one of his friends gave him the address of a farmer, an old country musician who was likely to have one. The fine old fellow's 1959 Les Paul was carefully laid out on his bed, and Gibbons happened to have the $250 from the sale of the car in his pocket. The deal was done straight away, and the guitar was duly dubbed the Pearly Gates, or Mistress Pearly Gates to its closest friends (in this instance, there was only one close friend).

Having found his Holy Grail, Gibbons used this Les Paul on all the band's albums and at all their concerts, until it became too precious to take with him on the road. Gibson then made a copy of it for him, a copy that was offered to the public in a very limited edition, but, despite that, Billy still refuses to part with the original, regardless of how much money is offered to him for it.

LES PAUL DERRIG

SLASH

THE COPY THAT BROUGHT THE ORIGINAL BACK INTO FASHION

IN THE LATE 1980S, GUITAR ROCK WAS UNDER SERIOUS THREAT, HEADING TOWARDS HUMDRUM NORMALITY AND A DRONING MONOTONY. It took the fearsome five of Guns N' Roses to put the famous threesome of sex, drugs, and rock 'n' roll back on the agenda and remind everyone that this was a style of music that could feel, and be, dangerous. On the guitar, a guitar hero the like of whom hadn't been seen since Jimmy Page, with whom he had in common flowing locks that covered their eyes and a Les Paul held low down, far too low by any normal measure. With his top hat and cigarette, Slash immediately embodied the daydreams of teenagers from the time, and he's still inspiring people to take up the guitar thirty years on.

An inveterate collector, Slash had numerous guitars, but the one with which he remains forever associated and whose sound is thought of as his is the Burst, the Les Paul Standard from 1958, 1959, or 1960. These three years are particularly treasured as vintage years for Gibson, and the models from that time are highly sought-after Holy Grails that sell for huge amounts of money. Slash did a lot to expose a whole new generation to the delights of the Burst, and the speculation in Bursts that occurred from that time onwards can be attributed to him. What's more, before this happened, Les Paul guitars were completely out of fashion, and it wasn't unusual to see guitarists trying to exchange them for Jacksons or Superstrats,

which were all the rage at the time. On top of that, Gibson had not yet started to re-release its Bursts at the frenetic pace it does today. Fans who didn't have the resources to find an original model therefore had to resort to copies made by independent luthiers. In a twist of fate, Slash's main Les Paul at the time when the first album *Appetite For Destruction* was recorded, and thus the one that caused all the uproar and led to Gibson's selling thousands of guitars, was just such a copy. The band was in the process of recording the album early in 1987. Slash, like a true junkie, had compiled a whole arsenal of equipment made up only of mediocre guitars that he hadn't managed to sell on. The band's manager, Alan Niven, anxious to ensure that his charges did some high-quality work, had set about looking for a good Les Paul and had managed to unearth two counterfeit Bursts created at the workshop of the Californian luthier Kris Derrig. Slash chose his favorite of the two, and the lucky winner was given a pair of Seymour Duncan Alinico Pro II pickups, for a more modern and compressed sound than the original PAF. The greatest irony of all was that Gibson released a replica of this copy in 2010, calling it the Slash Appetite Les Paul.

Slash in 2015 with ▶ his signature Rosso Corsa Epiphone.

AT THE OTHER END OF THE JACK

Slash brought an aging classic back into fashion on the amp front, too. At a time when most virtuoso guitarists swore by enormous digital rack amps, he made Marshall stack amps as cool as they had been in the days when Page plugged his Les Pauls into them. The model he liked most was the Silver Jubilee, a relatively rare model given that it was on sale for just one year, 1987, to celebrate the manufacturer's 25th anniversary. The guitar hero in the top hat defended the British maker's colors so well that he ended up being the first guitarist to be given a signature Marshall model, the famous JCM Slash from 1996. Since then, Marshall has released two more models signed by the master's hand, the AFD100 (featuring the 100-watt Plexi used to record *Appetite For Destruction*, hence the name) and the SL-5.

Slash on stage with ▶
Guns N' Roses in 1988.

THE BENCHMARK SOUND

GUNS· N' ROSES
"Mr. Brownstone"
Appetite For Destruction
(1987)

STRATOCASTER
YNGWIE MALMSTEEN
THE UGLY DUCKLING

*The famous Strat played by ▶
Yngwie Malmsteen,
reproduced by the
Fender Custom Shop.*

THE SWEDISH SHREDDER YNGWIE MALMSTEEN OFTEN COMES IN FOR FIERCE CRITICISM DUE TO HIS DIFFICULT PERSONALITY and his tendency to do down all other guitarists. For all that, his mastery of the instrument is unparalleled, and his choice of guitars is certainly out of the ordinary. Whereas most of the virtuosos from the 1980s swore by Superstrats and other guitars with highlighter colors, humbuckers, and Floyd Rose tremolo arms, Yngwie kept faith with his Stratocasters with pickups at the vintage output level in Marshall Plexis, a resolutely vintage configuration inspired mainly by his idol, Ritchie Blackmore.

When the guitarist set off for the United States in hopes of forging a career there, all he had with him was a pair of jeans and a 1972 Strat he had bought in his teens. He had scalloped it (hollowed out the wood between the frets on the fingerboard) to suit the lightning speed of his playing, something that was to remain a trademark feature of the signature model that Fender dedicated to him in the late 1980s. This white Strat yellowed somewhat over time, as Yngwie added his own decorative elements, such as multiple cigarette burns and several stickers: one of Donald Duck's head on the guitar's headstock, earning it the affectionate nickname of "The Duck," another with the motto "Play Loud" on the front of the body and, on the back, the horse from the Ferrari logo, Ferrari being a company for which the virtuoso had a special fondness.

It is this Strat that can be heard throughout the Viking's first album in 1984, and it can also be seen amid the flames on the album sleeve.

Later, Malmsteen would appear with numerous other Strats, but The Duck was to remain the most important of them all, and, according to the maestro himself, the one with the greatest sound. When you appreciate what a fine ear he has, you find yourself taking his word for it.

THE BENCHMARK SOUND

Yngwie J. Malmsteen's
Rising Force

**YNGWIE MALMSTEEN
"Far Beyond the Sun"
Rising Force (1984)**

*Yngwie Malmsteen in 2008 ▶
playing in front of a whole
wall of Marshall stack amps.*

JACKSON CONCORDE
RANDY RHOADS
THE FLYING V GETS ANGRY

◄ *The re-release of the Concorde by the Jackson Custom Shop, a limited edition of 25 guitars released in 2005 to mark the model's 25th anniversary.*

IN 1980, RANDY RHOADS JOINED THE BAND SET UP BY OZZY OSBOURNE, WHO HAD HIMSELF JUST BEEN THROWN OUT OF BLACK SABBATH, AND STARTED LOOKING FOR THE PERFECT GUITAR WITH WHICH TO REPLACE THE LES PAUL CUSTOM that he had played with such dazzling effect up until then. Randy put in a call to Grover Jackson, who at the time owned the firm Charvel, to discuss the version of the Flying V that he had in mind. He wanted a more pointed and extended body, one that was less imposing: it has to be said that the California native isn't the tallest guitarist in the world, and he almost used to disappear behind the giant proportions of the standard Flying V. The first prototype was a superb neck-thru white wing with gold appointments, whose ultra-modern shape earned it the nickname Concorde, after the supersonic jet plane.

Rhoads, though, wanted to go even further, and he urged Jackson to make the design more radical. Jackson eventually arrived at the Concorde 2, an even more pointed black guitar with sharktooth inlays that went on to become a classic of the 1980s. The guitar was so unusual that Jackson didn't want to associate it with Charvel, and so put his own name on it. And thus the Jackson firm was born, with the Randy Rhoads design still accounting for a large portion of the catalogue today.

HOHNER MADCAT PRINCE

NOT exactly a FENDER

HOHNER IS A GERMAN FIRM THAT MADE ITS NAME IN THE HARMONICA BUSINESS, BUT, IN THE 1970S, IT DECIDED TO GET INTO GUITARS and created some affordable models made in Japan. Among them was the Madcat, Hohner's version of the Telecaster. Before long, Fender caught wind of this illegal competitor (the headstock had exactly the same design as the Telecaster) and the model ceased production following a lawsuit.

It so happened that one of these very rare copies ended up in a guitar shop in Minneapolis, then made its way into the hands of one Prince Rogers Nelson in 1983, just before he exploded into the pop firmament with the hit album *Purple Rain*. Prince could have played any Telecaster whatsoever, yet he plumped for this Hohner... how are we to explain this? First of all, it must be said that Fender's manufacturing quality at the time was distinctly average, leaving ample room for high-quality copies. Secondly, the Madcat has a striking allure, with its leopard-print pickguard and its finish, which brings out the best in its gorgeous flame maple. Finally, Prince always did things his way, and no doubt reveled in this defiant difference.

Following the unexpected global exposure provided by Prince, which went well beyond their hopes, Hohner re-released the Madcat, only this time they made sure to alter the shape of the headstock.
Once bitten, twice shy.

FOLLOWING PAGES
Prince in 1995 with the guitar Love Symbol, which mirrors the design of his logo at the time. Another photo from 1984 for the Purple Rain *tour, this time with the guitar dubbed Cloud.*

▲
Prince with the famous Hohner during his Purple Rain *tour in 1984.*

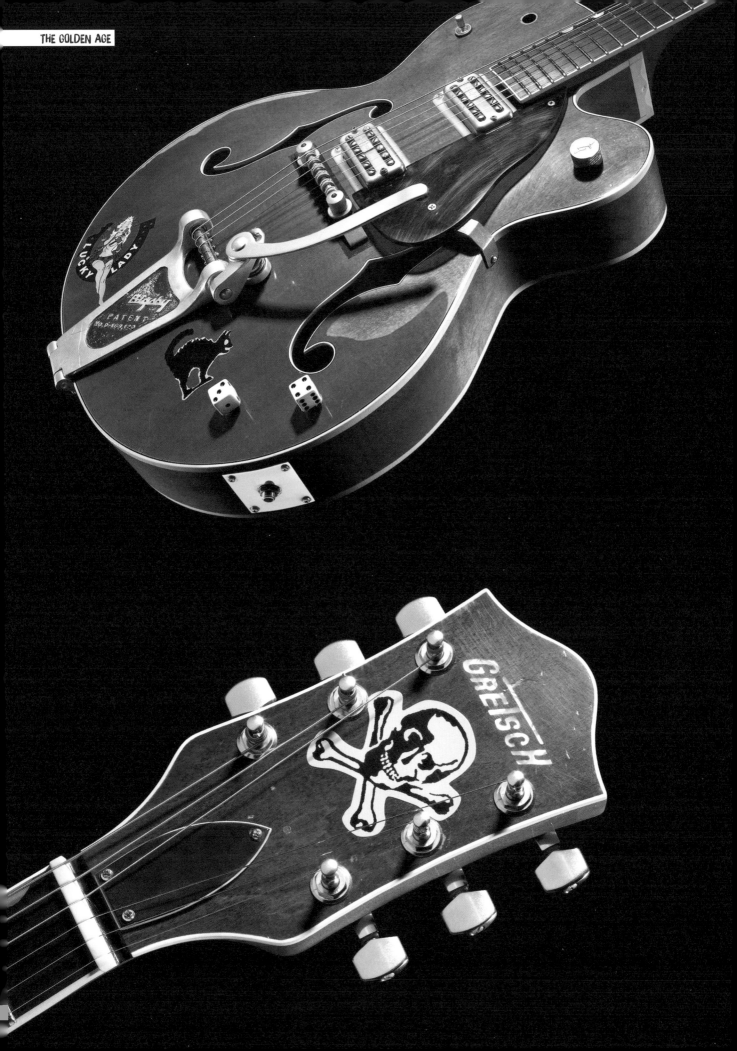

GRETSCH 6120
BRIAN SETZER

ROCKABILLY COMES BACK INTO FAVOR

◄ *The Gretsch Custom Shop's tribute to their best-ever representative, a limited edition of 59 guitars released in 2009.*

THE 1980S ARE A DECADE THAT WE TEND TO ASSOCIATE WITH SYNTHESIZERS AND RHYTHM BOXES, but they were also the decade during which nostalgia for the 1950s, reinvented, became a movement in its own right. Musically, the band that spearheaded the rockabilly revival was, of course, the trio The Stray Cats, whose first, eponymous album made a whole generation of punks in search of historic models hungry to get their hands on a Gretsch. With the singles "Rock This Town," "Runaway Boys," and "Stray Cat Strut," the trio of New Yorkers first of all made it big in the UK, before becoming legends in their own country. On the cover of the first album, Brian Setzer, the band's guitarist and singer, is seen holding a Gretsch 6120 dating from 1959. Gretsch guitars had gone completely out of fashion in 1981, but, like the true fan of Eddie Cochran that he was, Setzer had decided to appropriate this much-maligned model by decorating it with stickers typical of the hot rod movement: a black cat underneath the vibrato arm and a skull and crossbones on the headstock. On stage, the huge guitar almost concealed the scrawny guitarist, making him look even more like a cartoon character.

Straight away, everyone wanted a Gretsch, so much so that the label was brought back to life after a very alarming period of downtime. The 6120 thus became his signature model in 1990, the first in a very long line of Setzer models (the Gretsch

catalog now features no fewer than seven models signed by the maestro). In 2007, the Gretsch Custom Shop finally came full circle by reproducing the original 1959 guitar, down to the smallest details.

This superb exercise in style, of which just 59 copies were made, even featured the same stickers as the old 6120!

Poster from the time of ► *Brian Setzer's tour of Japan in 2002.*

IBANEZ SIGNATURE JOE SATRIANI

INSTRUMENTAL MUSIC FOR EVERYONE

JOE SATRIANI IS A GUITAR ICON AND A WONDERFUL ANOMALY, FOR HE IS THE LAST ARTIST TO HAVE ACHIEVED A SUBSTANTIAL NUMBER OF ALBUM SALES while playing instrumental music: his 1987 album, *Surfing With the Alien*, sold more than a million copies, achieving platinum status, and was nominated for a Grammy Award. As an instrumental guitarist, the guitar is his voice; he therefore needs an instrument that won't leave the crowds exhausted after two songs, with a warm, round, and compressed sound. He started out on a Telecaster, then moved on to a Les Paul Deluxe (with mini-humbuckers), and found a suitable tool in a Kramer Pacer, a Superstrat that was very fashionable at the time, on which he recorded the first two albums.

Following the buzz generated by *Surfing With the Alien*, however, Satriani was put in touch with Ibanez by his former student Steve Vai, and they invited him to design his own signature model. Contrary to what might have been expected from an instrumental guitarist, he did not move towards a shredder design, opting instead for an instrument that would allow him to showcase beautiful, simple melodies. The design remains similar to that of the Strat but the body is more rounded, and the guitar has a Floyd Rose vibrato arm and two DiMarzio humbucker pickups with a low level of output similar to vintage PAFs. The profile of the neck is relatively thick, more like a Strat from the 1960s than a Jackson. The precise, warm sound of the JS model can be heard on all Satch's albums in one form or another, for this Ibanez became a best-seller and to date there have been thirty-three different reincarnations of it!

Joe Satriani in the late 1980s, before he switched to the shaved head and sunglasses look. ▶

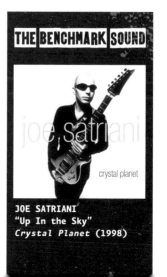

THE BENCHMARK SOUND

JOE SATRIANI
"Up In the Sky"
Crystal Planet (1998)

THE MODERN AGE

GRUNGE AND ALTERNATIVE ROCK

172

FROM METAL TO DJENT

194

GUITAR HEROES OF THE FUTURE

218

Jag-Stang
KURT COBAIN
THE LOVABLE MONSTER

▲
The production model of the Jag-Stang, the result of Kurt Cobain's brilliant design.

NIRVANA'S FRONT-MAN IS ONE OF THE GUITAR HEROES OF TRULY GREAT STATURE, EVEN THOUGH, BEING A MUSICIAN FROM THE UNDERGROUND, HE WOULD HAVE VEHEMENTLY REJECTED THE DESCRIPTION. The fact remains that he inspired a whole generation to start playing, and any guitarist currently in their thirties certainly owes something to him. Kurt Cobain's relationship to his instrument was very ambiguous, since, in the manner of Pete Townshend, most of his guitars ended up smashed to pieces at the end of concerts whose savagery knew no bounds. His punk ethic and his limited resources pushed him towards affordable instruments like the Jaguar or the Mustang, two models made by Fender whose shape was known as "offset" (like the Jazzmaster), guitars for which there was so little demand at the time that they were no longer being manufactured. Their price tags therefore tended to be very small, and Kurt Cobain was quick to modify them so that they suited him perfectly, on the one hand by turning them into instruments for left-handers if he happened to have found a right-handed instrument, and on the other hand by fitting a humbucker on the bridge, a pickup far more suited to the torrents of distortion in grunge music than the original small, single-coil pickup.

In 1993, Nirvana were at the peak of their fame, with the financial resources that came with that. Cobain therefore asked the Fender Custom Shop to make a unique hybrid of his two favorite models. He gave them a Polaroid collage of a Jaguar and a Mustang assembled using scotch tape, leaving the imagination of the luthiers Mark Kendrick and Larry Brooks to do the rest. The result, the Jag-Stang, was a completely new design. For Cobain, however, even this unique object remained nothing more than a tool, which he immediately set about modifying as he saw fit. The lovable monster survived its creator's suicide and remained in the Fender catalogue from 1995 to 2001.

THE BENCHMARK SOUND

NIRVANA
"Drain You" [1991]
From the Muddy Banks Of the Wishkah (1996)

Kurt Cobain on stage ▶
on December 13, 1993,
for the filming of "Live and Loud" on MTV.

ELECTRICAL GUITAR COMPANY
BUZZ OSBORNE
Metal on metal

BUZZ OSBORNE iS THE ARCHETYPAL GuiTAR ANTiHERO, A MONUMENT TO THE UNDERGROUND light-years away from the megalomaniacal trip of the traditional rock soloist. Yet, as the founder and leader of the Melvins, his riffs have influenced countless great musicians since 1987, including a certain Kurt Cobain. To achieve the band's enormous guitar sound, so thick and oily that the Melvins' style has been described as "sludge rock," Osborne for a long time played a Gibson Les Paul Custom, a Black Beauty as heavy in the sound as on the shoulders. The only drawback was the neck of these models — it was too wide for King Buzzo's little hands — along with their fragility when faced with the rigors of the road and a style of playing that was physical, to say the least.

In 2010, with the help of his friends from the band Isis, Osborne discovered the manufacturer Electrical Guitar Company, a small workshop specializing in guitars made entirely of aluminum. The advantage of aluminum is that thickness is not required in order to obtain stability, by contrast with wood: it was therefore very easy for the manufacturer to shape the neck so that it was super-slim, the shape Buzz dreamed of. As far as the scale and pickups were concerned, he stayed true to what had already been installed on his Les Paul. While the Gibson 498T and 490R pickups may not be favorites among fans of vintage accessories, their brutal level of output seemed to fit what he was looking for. As counter-intuitive as it may seem, making an instrument out of aluminum does not produce a brighter, shinier sound — the opposite is true, and Buzzo seemed to love the extra bass notes that his new instrument of choice provided. Electrical Guitar Company eventually released a King Buzzo Standard model that the artist duly takes on tour with him, whereas the Les Paul stays at home.

◄ *Buzz Osborne on stage with the Melvins in 2012.*

GUILD S-100
KIM THAYIL
THE OTHER SG

KIM THAYIL IS THE GUITARIST OF SOUNDGARDEN, THE LED ZEPPELIN OF GRUNGE. IN THE SEATTLE BAND, HE ASSERTED HIS VERY DISTINCTIVE STYLE consisting of excellent mastery of open tunings and a fondness for eclectic and original sonic ambiences. He took up the guitar midway between the punk explosion of the 1970s and the hardcore of the 1980s, two movements whose DIY and anti-conformist philosophy never left him. When the time came to pick his first serious guitar in 1978, he duly opted for a Guild S-100. Guild is an American manufacturer that started out by designing outstanding acoustic guitars, before shifting towards the electric side of things. The S-100 is very obviously inspired by the SG Gibson, whose shape it recreates (albeit with a higher upper horn) as well as its pickup configuration with two humbuckers. Thayil no doubt chose the Guild for several reasons: the price, first and foremost, significantly lower than the Gibson's; the slimmer neck; and the fact that he was able to scratch behind the bridge on the bass string side, for as much of a noise effect as anyone could want. The overriding suspicion, however, is that he wanted to stand out from the crowd, something he definitely succeeded in doing, because even today, the model is inextricably associated with him.

Kim Thayil in 2013, loyal to his Guild.
▼

G&L RAMPAGE
JERRY CANTRELL
THE UNEXPECTED ONE

▲
*Jerry Cantrell in 2009,
with his Rampage.*

WHEN WE HEAR THE ENORMOUS,
LUMBERING GUITAR ON ALICE IN CHAINS,
IT'S EASY TO PICTURE THE BAND'S
RIFFER-IN-CHIEF, JERRY CANTRELL, holding
a Les Paul in his hands. And while it's true
that he was also known to strum on the
Gibson Black Beauty, he is even more
associated with a little-known model that he
took towards a musical horizon for which it
hadn't necessarily been designed.

In 1979, Leo Fender teamed up with George
Fullerton (another of the architects of
Fender) to found G&L (George and Leo), a
firm that enabled Fender to overtake its
original creations so as to adapt them for the
market of the day. Rather than create yet
another Stratocaster, they took another look
at the model's curves and christened it the
Rampage, while fitting it, for all the would-be
Van Halens, with a Kahler vibrato arm (Floyd
Rose's main competitor) and a single
humbucker pickup designed by Schaller.
Cantrell got his hands on a Rampage in 1984,
and customized it by changing the pickup to a
Seymour Duncan SH4, a real classic when it
comes to big sound. He then made it truly
unique with the help of a huge sticker of a
pin-up model in a blue dress, a painting by
Alain Aslan created for the French magazine
Oui, and a "Rock 'n' Roll" sticker positioned
under the strings. Thus the guitar nicknamed
"Blue Dress" could tick off both sex and rock
'n' roll, and the bands soon took care of the
third ingredient on the list as well.

JAZZMASTER SONIC YOUTH
THE ART OF NOISE

◀ *The Fender Lee Ranaldo Signature Jazzmaster.*

ROCK ISN'T SOLELY THE DOMAIN OF HAIR-BRAINED LUNATICS — A CERTAIN AMOUNT OF FINESSE HAS A ROLE TO PLAY TOO. What's more, rock has an artistic avant-garde of its own in the shape of the two guitarists from Sonic Youth, Lee Ranaldo and Thurston Moore. Never once have the pair played a traditional piece with normal tuning, and their trademark is inventing open tunings that correspond to each piece, to the extent that they end up going through dozens of instruments to avoid endless pauses during their concerts. They are also pioneers when it comes to using worked-up guitars, modified using everyday objects to obtain sounds that sound like anything but a guitar. Out of a concern for sturdiness and dependability, they have always used Fenders, particularly Telecaster Deluxe models (with two Wide Range humbuckers designed by Fender in the 1970s), Jaguars and Mustangs. Then, in the late 1980s, they were introduced to the Jazzmaster via their friend J Mascis. The scale, longer than that of the two other offsets, immediately made the guitar perfect for maintaining good string tension, but the complicated electronics didn't suit them. They therefore began a huge simplification process, retaining only the volume knob and the pickup selector switch. Out of habit, they replaced the original pickups with Wide Ranges, and, to gain greater reliability, the original bridge made way for a Gibson-style Tune-O-Matic or a Mustang bridge. Made-to-measure

instruments modified in this way were affectionately dubbed "Jazzblasters." In 2009, Fender released a model of the Jazzmaster for each of the two musicians, including all their modifications. Fans of Sonic Youth can't have been the only ones who felt the Jazzblaster was right up their street, for the two guitars quickly became best-sellers, even helping to bring the original back to center stage.

Lee Ranaldo at the Primavera ▶
Sound Festival
in Barcelona in 2013.
Thurston Moore at the Bime
Festival in 2014 in Bilbao.

SQUIER SIGNATURE JAZZMASTER
J MASCIS
FROM VINTAGE TO LOW BUDGET

WHEN J MASCIS SET UP THE TRIO DINOSAUR JR. IN 1984, IT'S FAIR TO SAY THE JAZZMASTER WAS JUST ABOUT THE LEAST COOL INSTRUMENT you could find in a store, a has-been relic from the golden age of surf music. Fender had even stopped producing the model in 1980, and after that, models made in the 1960s, which would now be considered vintage, became available for next to nothing in pawnshops. The peroxide-blond stars of MTV didn't play Jazzmasters; it would take a real nerd, weirdo, or freak, like the anti-hero J Mascis, to choose such a gizmo. Until then, everyone saw them as machines for making a bright, clear sound that was a little on the shrill side, but, as J Mascis proved, they can also handle themselves very well indeed when faced with an enormous wall of fuzz sound.

To make them ideally suited to his curmudgeonly style, J Mascis typically makes three alterations to all the vintage Jazzmasters he can find: the small original frets are replaced with jumbo ones for a better grip, the electronic circuit is simplified, and the original bridge is replaced with the very reliable Tune-O-Matic. As the vintage market evolved, these instruments became ever more desirable, making them far too expensive for most of the band's fans. J Mascis, ever anxious to preserve the underground spirit in which the band came into being, therefore decided to design a signature Japanese model. In 2007, this bizarre violet Jazzmaster with a Tune-O-

Matic bridge was released, but before long the price tag put on it by the Japanese manufacturer shot up, and the guitar once again became unaffordable.

In 2011, therefore, J Mascis presented a model that he produced with Squier, this time in white with a gold pickguard (and a Tune-O-Matic, as ever), a model costing less than $500 that he regularly plays on stage alongside vintage models worth over $5,000. In the end, it's our actions that really count.

◄ The Japanese Fender
J Mascis signature
Jazzmaster.

VOLUME

TONE

5 SIGNATURE MODELS THAT WON'T BREAK THE BANK

THE IDEA BEHIND SIGNATURE MODELS IS AS SIMPLE AS IT GETS: WE ALL WANT TO IMITATE OUR IDOLS WHEN WE FIRST START PLAYING THE GUITAR, AND CHOOSING A GUITAR THAT BEARS THE SEAL OF APPROVAL OF ONE OF THESE MASTERS IS BOTH REASSURING AND MOTIVATING. VERY OFTEN, THOUGH, THE STARS PLAY TOP-OF-THE-LINE INSTRUMENTS THAT PROVE TO BE OUT OF REACH FOR MODEST BUDGETS. SO WHENEVER THE PROS MAKE THE EFFORT TO DESIGN AN REASONABLY-PRICED INSTRUMENT THAT ISN'T JUST A PROMOTIONAL TOOL, CHANCES ARE IT'S GOING TO BE A PRETTY INTERESTING GUITAR.

◄ PRS SE ORIANTHI (2010)

Orianthi garnered a colossal amount of exposure when the film This Is It came out, since she was part of the group who rehearsed with Michael Jackson in the lead-up to the King of Pop's dramatic return to the stage. Since then, the Australian has released a solo album and played the role of flamboyant guitarist for another legendary singer, Alice Cooper. Previously, Carlos Santana had already given it as a gift to Paul Reed Smith (PRS), who endorsed it and ended up dedicating this signature model to him. Recognizing that numerous women were inspired to take up the guitar by Orianthi, the firm designed a very high-quality guitar that was accessible to serious female beginners.

▲ FENDER JIMMIE VAUGHAN TEX-MEX STRAT (1996)

Jimmie Vaughan is the older brother of Stevie Ray, and whisper it quietly, but connoisseurs will tell you that his was the greater talent, even though SRV achieved a far greater level of fame. In addition to an exciting solo career, Jimmie Vaughan also played guitar for the Fabulous Thunderbirds. When he designed his signature Stratocaster, he specified that he wanted it to be made in Mexico, so that it would be as widely accessible as possible. At the time, most affordable signature models were variations on high-end models, but the Jimmie Vaughan only ever existed in this version.

SQUIER J MASCIS ▶ JAZZMASTER (2011)

From a distance, it's impossible to say with certainty that this very inexpensive Jazzmaster isn't a vintage model from 1959, the first year of production, which used the gold pickguard that J Mascis chose for his Squier model. Even when it's in your hands, the Mascis doesn't disappoint, such is the similarity between its resonance and that of the extremely expensive originals. And the pickups, usually the Achilles' heel of guitars in this price-range, have an interesting personality that can really be worked with. What's more, the Tune-O-Matic bridge allows for better stability. So, does it represent guitar perfection? It's certainly pretty close.

EPIPHONE JOE BONAMASSA ▶ FIREBIRD I (2016)

Joe Bonamassa has put his name to a prodigious number of signature models, but this one is without question the most interesting of the lot. It is a replica of the guitar that he nicknamed Treasure, a Firebird I from 1963. Firebirds from that era are extremely rare, and the handful of re-editions of the Firebird offered by Gibson or Epiphone recreate the more readily available Firebird III or V. With its single pickup, Treasure embraces the style of an instrument tailor-made for rock, and, at the price of an Epiphone, you can take it down to the bar at the end of the road without having to worry about protecting it from any tiny scratch or bump.

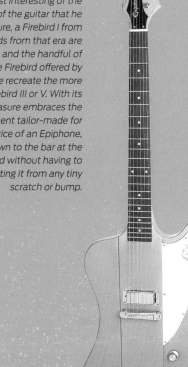

IBANEZ PAUL GILBERT FRM100 (2011)

In 2009, Paul Gilbert, the brilliant shredder from Mr. Big and Racer X, designed an Ibanez model very different from his customary signature RG. He took the body of the Iceman, turned it upside down, and it was then that the idea of the Fireman came to him (ice and fire being opposites). The PGM FRM1 was a very high-end model, but two years later, the FRM100 enabled even the most impoverished fans to have a go as well. The FRM100 is more than just a cheaper model, though, as its body is made of mahogany as opposed to the FRM1's korina, two radically different substances for sonic characters that complement one another.
▼

KIT WARMOTH
RIVERS CUOMO
THE STRAT WITH THE LIGHTNING STRAP

THE BAND WEEZER ENJOYED CONSIDERABLE SUCCESS WITH THEIR EPONYMOUS FIRST ALBUM IN 1994. IT WASN'T GRUNGE MUSIC, THOUGH, and front-man Rivers Cuomo had more of the look of Buddy Holly, or a geeky programmer, about him than the all-enveloping charisma of a Cobain. But the songs were excellent, and so the public accepted everything else that went with them. And that "everything else" included instruments that obeyed the golden rule of punk: Do It Yourself. When they recorded their first album, Cuomo played the producer's guitars, and for the next tour he personally assembled a guitar using spare parts purchased by mail order from a Warmoth catalog.

The end product was a baby-blue hardtail Strat with two humbucker pickups: a Seymour Duncan on the bridge and a DiMarzio on the neck. This unlikely look was rendered even more unusual by the fact that the two pickups were different colors, and the blue beauty was paired with a black strap adorned with white lightning. Once assembled, this creation followed Rivers on stage, playing its role as a musical tool to perfection: it never went out of tune, the strings didn't break, and Cuomo went on using the guitar until 2000 even though it took a nasty blow to the body in 1997, one that left a long crack from one end to the other, which was hastily papered over with an impressive array of stickers.

Cuomo eventually replaced it with other guitars assembled in the same way, but also with more standard instruments that nicely illustrate the band's musical wanderings. Then, at last, in 2014, Cuomo went back to his first love and made it the symbol of the band's return to its origins on the artistic front. In "Back To the Shack," he sings: "Let's get back, back to the shack, back to the Strat with the lightning strap." When we're in the grip of a romance...

◄ *Rivers Cuomo in concert in 2016, after returning to the famous Strat from the band's early days.*

BILLIE JOE ARMSTRONG

THE BRAT OF ROCK 'N' ROLL

THE PUNK REVOLUTION OF 1977 WAS A SHORT-LIVED AFFAIR, AND ITS HEROES HAVE NOW DISAPPEARED. SOME TWENTY YEARS LATER, THOUGH, in 1994, the movement got its second wind on the other side of the world, in California, where a whole generation of pimply teenagers with piercings everywhere found themselves in the battle against materialism and the Do It Yourself ethic of the original punks. Spearheading this assault were none other than the trio Green Day, who sold more than 20 million copies of the album *Dookie* (1994), after it was propelled up the charts by the single "Basket Case."

As guitarist and vocalist, Billie Joe Armstrong adhered to the basic rules of the punk ethic by only ever playing one guitar, a copy of a Strat that was in fact the first electric he had ever had, given to him when he was 11 years old. This Fernandes was dubbed simply "Blue" in a nod to its original color, which can just be made out underneath the legion of stickers that were put on it. Billie Joe inscribed his initials in red on the white pickguard, and the bridge pickup was replaced with a humbucker, the great classic Seymour Duncan SH-4 Jeff Beck.

After having used and abused this guitar to his heart's content, Armstrong began to take an interest in Gibson's Les Paul Junior, a punk instrument if ever there was one because it was a model made for beginners, costing far less than the Standard and Custom models. There were two different versions of the Junior: a single cutaway model, Leslie West style, from 1954 to 1958, then a double cutaway model, Keith Richards style, from 1958 to 1960. Green Day's riffer was initially interested in the first version, so much so that Gibson made a signature model for him after the enormous success of *American Idiot* in 2004 (14 million albums, truly a second career high, ten years on from the first one). It is still one of the models most faithful to the Junior from that time, without the would-be owner's having to shell out the sizeable price of a Custom Shop replica or an original. His second signature model created less hype and it was simply the second version of the Junior, with double cutaways.

In spite of this attraction to other instruments, up until the superb black Les Paul Custom of which abundant use was made on *Revolution Radio* (2016), Billie Joe never strays far from his first love. Blue always goes on the road with the band, in its original form and in the form of replicas dreamed up by Fender. It has seen so much service that its maple fingerboard has turned from yellow to grey.

GREEN DAY
"American Idiot"
American Idiot (2004)

Billie Joe Armstrong ▶ on stage in 2009, still accompanied by Blue.

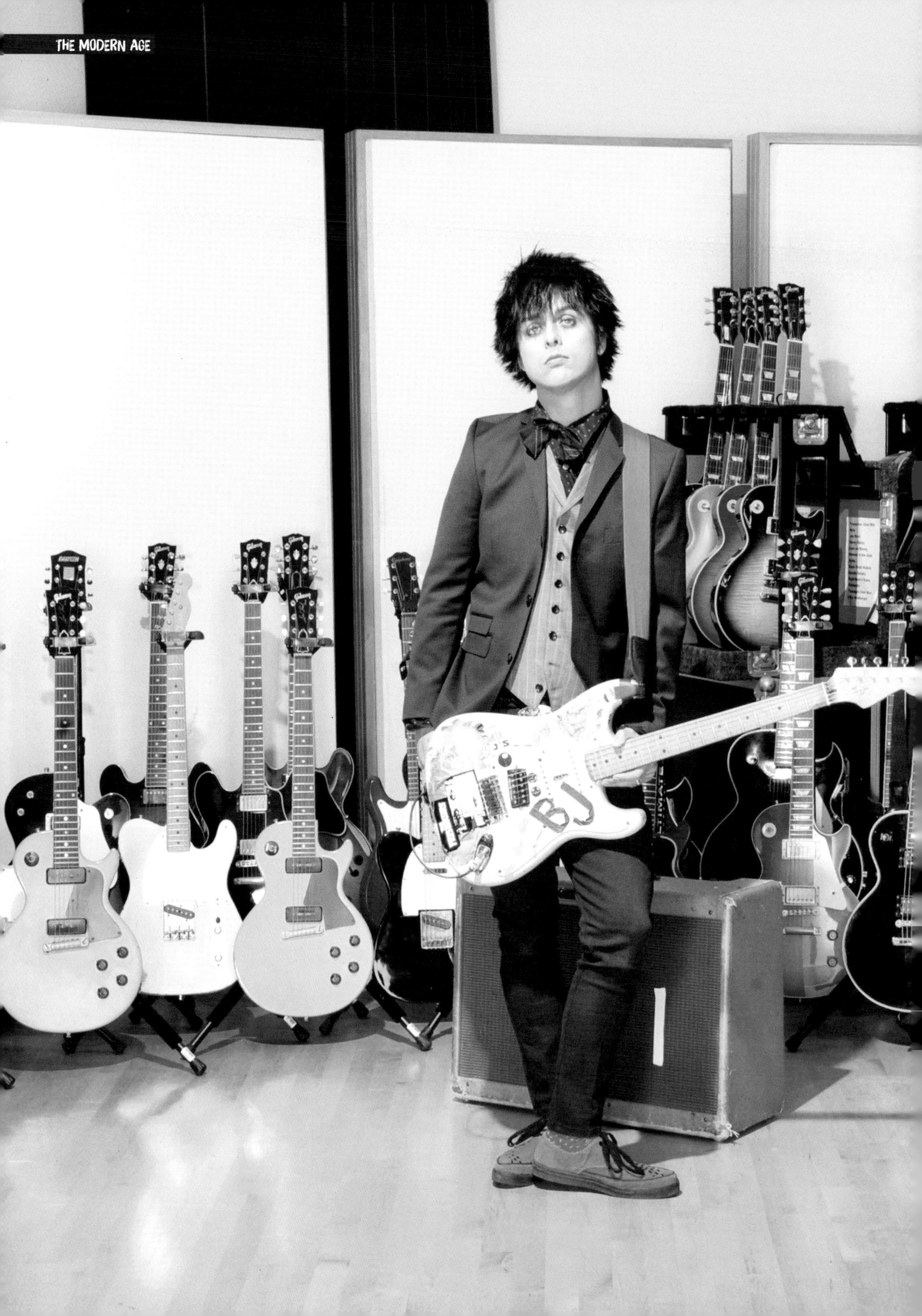
BJ

EVERLY FOR EVER

Unlike most punks, who are only interested in electricity and massive distortion, Billie Joe Armstrong is also passionate about acoustic guitars, even though this facet of his playing is only rarely expressed in Green Day. When he allows himself to take a break away from his amp, he does so on a Gibson Everly Brothers. This signature model in honor of the famous duo has the base of a J-185 (a J-200 with a smaller body) with a double pickguard, a black finish, and star-shaped fingerboard inlays. The Gibson Billie Joe Armstrong J-180 recreates these specs, adding an electro-acoustic sensor for the stage. What's more, such is the punk hero's love of his folk brethren that he teamed up with Norah Jones to record an album consisting entirely of covers of Everly Brothers hits, *Foreverly*, in 2013. The album slipped under the radar but is well worth a listen.

THE BENCHMARK SOUND

BILLIE JOE + NORAH
foreverly

BILLIE JOE ARMSTRONG
AND NORAH JONES
"That Silver Haired Daddy
Of Mine"
Foreverly (2013)

◀ *Billie Joe Armstrong
and his collection.*

189

KIT
TOM MORELLO
MR. DIY

IN 1986, TOM MORELLO HAD JUST ARRIVED IN HOLLYWOOD, SEEKING, AS SO MANY OTHERS HAD DONE, TO PURSUE HIS DREAM OF MAKING A LIVING FROM MUSIC, but his lack of funds prevented him from using high-quality instruments. He therefore went along to the Performance Guitar store, a workshop that sold guitars put together using spare parts, so as to design his ultimate guitar there, one that he could use for all his projects. Once he had the result in his hands, he was disappointed: it didn't sound like he wanted it to, the sensations weren't right, and even the look of it wasn't really to his liking. Lacking the finances to be able to replace it, he hit upon the idea of doing some DIY work on this ersatz Strat, until he achieved what he had been hoping for.

He went through numerous replacement necks before finding one that really suited him, a cheap copy of a Kramer with no visible marks on it. The pickups caused a great deal of wavering too, before his choice fell on EMGs, and the vibrato arm was initially a Floyd Rose, then a Kahler, before an Ibanez Lo-Pro Edge finally won out. Morello also took care of the decoration by hand-painting some hippos on the front of the guitar, as these were the only thing he could draw. Despite all these modifications, Morello still wasn't satisfied with the result, and it was then that he had another revelation: the instrument wasn't as important as what you did with it. He therefore decided to play without asking himself too many questions, and the tart sound that resulted was exactly what he needed for Rage Against the Machine's enormous riffs. The band was ultra-politicized, and, prior to a concert in 1993, Morello decorated his Strat with the slogan "Arm The Homeless." The phrase then became the guitar's nickname. The ghost of Woody Guthrie was no doubt hovering somewhere nearby.

"I DON'T REALLY LOOK AT THE GUITAR AS SOMETHING THAT DOES SLAVE LABOR, IT'S MORE OF A COLLEAGUE."

*Tom Morello in 2016 ▶
during a concert by his
band Prophets of Rage.*

PRECISION BASS RELIC
DON WAS
PATIENT ZERO

DON WAS IS THE ONLY BASSIST INCLUDED IN THIS WORK, FOR THE VERY GOOD REASON THAT HE WAS THE MAN BEHIND A REVOLUTION from which countless guitarists have benefited: the relic trend. Relic is the marketing term used by the Fender Custom Shop to denote the pre-aged instruments that it produces in order to imitate beautiful vintage guitars. The rationale was simple: Fenders from the 1950s and 1960s were so valuable that it no longer made sense to take them on tour, but the new models lacked the weathered veneer, scars, and alluring wear and tear that old guitars have. Romanticism on the one hand, functionality on the other. With artificial aging, Fender infused a poetic dimension into the production of new guitars and enabled pro guitarists to take to the stage with instruments that looked more realistic than the originals themselves.

Of course, trying to work out where the first relic came from is a futile task, but one thing's for sure: the driving force behind the project was Don Was. At the time, in 1994, he was the producer of *Voodoo Lounge*, the first Rolling Stones album that didn't feature their original bassist Bill Wyman. Among Richards' and Wood's impressive collection, he noticed a 1950s Telecaster that belonged to the latter, with a pickguard that looked old, although it had been made only recently. This technique gave him the idea of asking the Fender Custom Shop to make a prematurely aged bass for him, a Precision Bass with a rosewood fingerboard of the kind made in the 1960s.

The luthier Vince Cunetto was charged with making the guitar look aged. Off the back of this sale, the Custom Shop decided in 1995 to offer a limited edition of 100 Relic NoCasters (the Tele made in 1951) and 250 Relic Strats, and the idea was such a big hit that it eventually offered this service on all its regular models. Even today, this option accounts for the majority of all orders.

Don Was in the middle of a ▶ recording session, on a vintage Vox bass.

Dean ML
DIMEBAG DARRELL
A Fan Guitar...FOR THE FANS

THERE ARE SOME DREAMS THAT COME TRUE IN A WAY WE COULD NEVER HAVE HOPED FOR: IN 1981, WHEN HE WAS JUST 15 YEARS OLD, A CERTAIN DARRELL LANCE ABBOTT (WHO WOULD GO ON TO BECOME DIMEBAG) DREAMED OF HAVING A DEAN GUITAR.

At the time, these guitars were a very attractive alternative to those made by the big manufacturers, who missed the boat several times when it came to design. The Dean ML has a shape that really pushes the boundaries, very much inspired by the Gibson Explorer, but is a fine example of top-quality guitar-making. And it was this particular model that Darrell won in a competition, after a rendition of Van Halen's "Eruption."

That very morning, his father had bought him another one as a surprise present — the same model but in a different color. With his wish having come true not once but twice, Darrell ended up selling the ML from the competition a year later, so that he could buy a car with the proceeds. The luthier who took ownership of it modified it with a Floyd Rose vibrato arm and a custom midnight blue painted finish with white lightning.

With the ML as his go-to guitar in the band Pantera (he used a sunburst model for many years), Dimebag got into the habit of tracking down Deans in pawnshops in order to modify and restore them. After a stroke of luck, he ended up buying back the ML from the competition, and at that point he swore he would never part company again with the

guitar that now inherited the name "Dean From Hell," and to which two major adjustments were made so that it fully satisfied Dime's expectations: a new set of pickups (the very aggressive Bill Lawrence L-500XL on the bridge, the softer and more bluesy Seymour Duncan '59 on the neck), and above all a sticker depicting the band Kiss, of which he was a fan throughout his life, and that echoed his most famous tattoo. As he played more and more concerts, he also added some electrical tape to the sides of the bass pickup (so that the strings wouldn't get stuck when attacked with vigor), and he added notches to the knobs using a welding iron so that they wouldn't be slippery, even when his fingers were dripping with sweat. All these details are, of course included on the numerous guitars offered by Dean to fans of the brilliant Abbott.

◄ *Dimebag Darrell on stage in 1995, when Pantera's popularity was at its zenith.*

IBANEZ JEM
STEVE VAI

IDIOSYNCRATIC

IN 1986, STEVE VAI WAS THE GUITAR HERO TO END ALL GUITAR HEROES: HAVING LEARNED HIS TRADE IN FRANK ZAPPA'S BAND, HE WAS THE GUITARIST CHOSEN BY DAVID LEE ROTH FOR HIS FIRST post-Van Halen album, *Eat 'Em and Smile*.

As a result, he was given a huge amount of media exposure, and became a prime target for guitar makers keen to find credible ambassadors. In those days, Vai played heavily modified Strats, so he had a very specific idea of what he was looking for. He therefore sent a list of specifications to several makers, who confined themselves to making small adjustments to the models they already had in their catalogs. The only guitar maker that stood out was the Japanese firm Ibanez, whose prototype was very close to what Vai had dreamed about.

Taking a Strat with a highly unusual shape as the foundation, Vai designed a deeper cutaway on the treble side, for improved access to the final notes; four frets on the fingerboard are scalloped, for the same reason; the pickups are made by DiMarzio; and a cut-out section behind the Floyd Rose makes it possible to pull the notes upwards to an extreme. Finally, Vai wanted a guitar that would be instantly recognizable, and so he came up with the monkey grip, a cut-out in the upper part of the body that served as a handle for brandishing the guitar on stage, and that had the side-effect of making it lighter, since it obviously involved taking some wood out of the guitar.

After several adjustments, the end result was finally presented in 1987 and is known as the JEM777, available in three perfectly flashy highlighter colors. The disappearing pyramid inlays and the color scheme (fluorescent yellow with pink pickups and fluorescent green knobs, for example) make the model immediately recognizable. But whereas Vai and Ibanez thought that the JEM would serve as a way of getting exposure for the maker first and foremost, the model in fact became a best-seller, to the point that ten different versions can be found in the Ibanez catalog for 2017, thirty years after it was first launched.

With a view to making the JEM more democratic, Ibanez released the RG, a series of guitars recreating the shape and resolutely metal character of the original, minus the eccentric bits of decoration, and once again it was a bigger hit than anyone could possibly have expected. In the 1990s, the RG was the second-highest seller, behind the Strat.

NEXT DOUBLE-PAGE SPREAD
Steve Vai and his Universe Swirl in 1995.

Steve Vai live in 2016, ▶ during the tour for the album Modern Primitive.

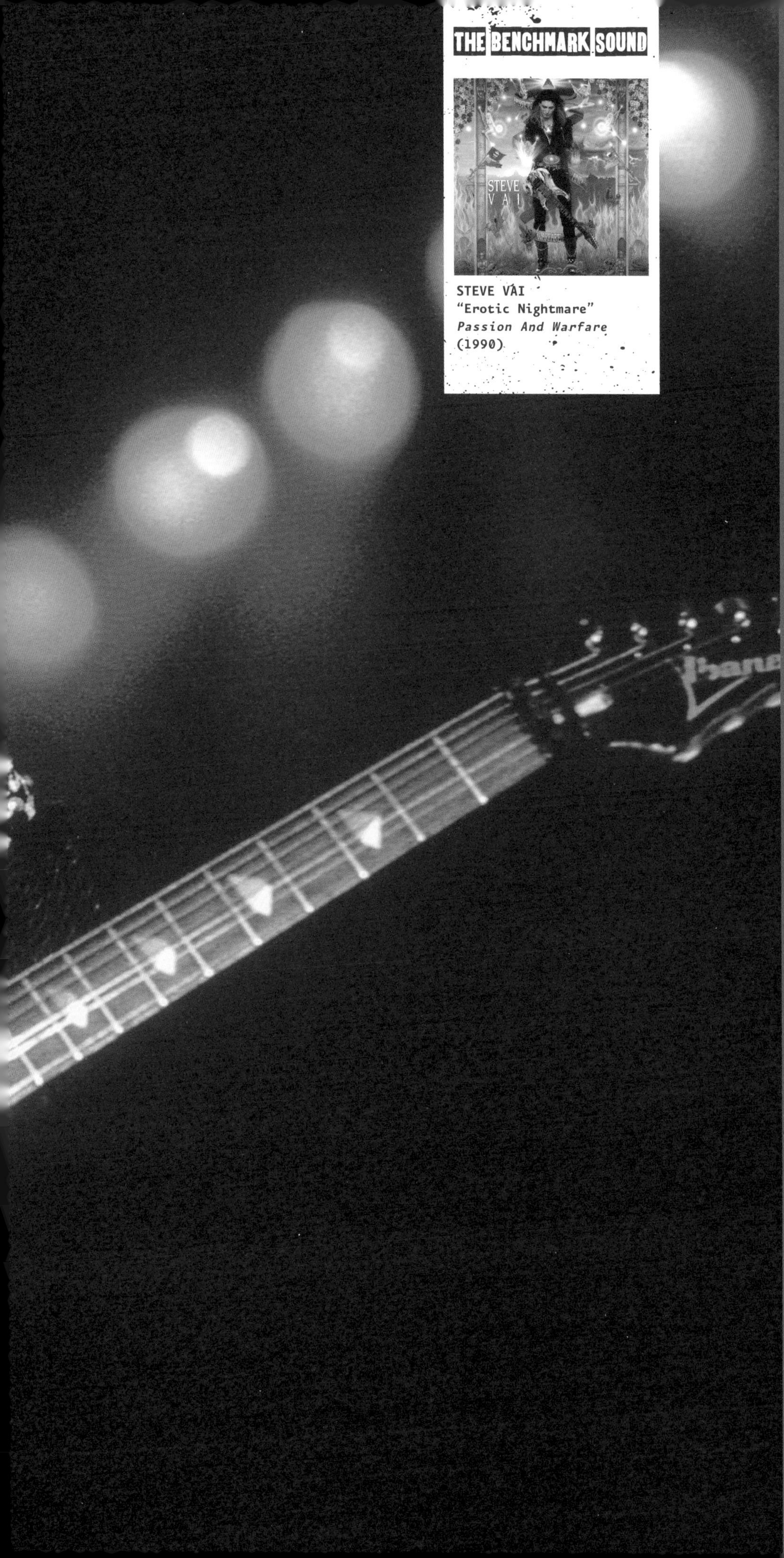

THE BENCHMARK SOUND

STEVE VAI
"Erotic Nightmare"
Passion And Warfare
(1990)

MASTER OF THE UNIVERSE

The idea of a seven-string guitar has been around for a long time: it's possible to find Gretsch guitars offering this option, designed for jazz players, which date from the 1960s. Be that as it may, the enormous success enjoyed by this design today can be traced back to an idea that Vai came up with. In 1989, he asked Ibanez to make a seven-string model for him, so that he could create bass-string riffs for the Whitesnake album *Slip Of the Tongue*. This collaboration resulted in the Universe model, the first seven-string guitar to have been designed for metal, with the radical shape of the JEM, a Floyd Rose, and the now-classic two humbucker/one single-coil configuration. In 1990, the virtuoso released his masterpiece, *Passion & Warfare*, posing with a Universe on the cover. The model was not quite the runaway success that the JEM had been, so much so that in 1995, Ibanez didn't produce a single Universe. However, *Awake* by Dream Theater came out in 1994, followed by *Demanufacture* by Fear Factory in 1995, and above all *Life Is Peachy* by Korn became the totemic album for a whole generation in 1996. All of these bands can clearly be heard making use of the Universe for their very deep, heavy riffs. Ibanez therefore became the benchmark brand for the seven-string guitar, which triumphed as the go-to instrument in the run-up to the new millennium.

GIBSON EXPLORER
James Hetfield
THE EXPLORER FINDS ITS PLACE

WHEN THE CALIFORNIAN OUTFIT METALLICA RELEASED ITS FIRST ALBUM *KILL 'EM ALL* **IN 1983, THE WORLD DISCOVERED A NEW STYLE OF MUSIC** that it didn't even know existed, a brutal blend of punk, heavy metal, and Motorhead. This super-charged cocktail was called thrash metal, and the new style immediately found a figurehead in a certain James Hetfield. Metallica's frontman is an unrivaled rhythm guitarist capable of stacking up rip-roaring riffs without any sign of fatigue, as well as a singer with the charisma required of a frontman and intimidating stature: he stands six foot one. Given his height and his playing technique (he doesn't play solos and attacks almost exclusively downwards, therefore holding his instrument very low), the Gibson Explorer was a natural fit for him. Until that point, few artists had touched the enormous contraption, but it looked perfectly natural in Hetfield's hands, and thus became an object of desire for the new generation of metalheads.

He bought his first new model in 1984, for the recording of *Ride the Lightning*, opting for the white version. After that, most of the guitars he used on stage were either white or black. The Explorer has a large body, so in order to take control of the big empty white space, Hetfield wrote "So What" on it in black letters, a reference to the song by the punk outfit Anti-Nowhere League. As for his reserve guitar, virtually identical, it had the demand "More Beer" emblazoned on it. In 1987, the band's sound became colder and more trenchant, in keeping with Hetfield's transition to active EMG pickups, which are still his favorite pickups thirty years later. That was also the time when he was approached by the Japanese manufacturer ESP, and the first model he requested was, of course, a white Explorer. ESP now offers eleven Hetfield models, including four white Explorers and three black ones. Seek the natural look...

James Hetfield in 1988 ▶
on the "Monsters
of Rock" tour.

LES PAUL CUSTOM
ZAKK WYLDE
THE BANNER

◄ *Zakk Wylde strikes a pose in 1999: note the extreme amount of bend on the low E string.*

ZAKK WYLDE IS ONE OF THE FEW MUSICIANS TO HAVE REMAINED FAITHFUL TO A LES PAUL EVEN WHEN THE CLASSIC MODEL WAS IN FREE FALL. He joined Ozzy Osbourne's band in 1987, accompanied right from the outset by the instrument that was to remain closely associated with him, a Les Paul Custom modified with active EMG 81 (bridge) and 85 (neck) pickups for his more brutal, precise, and modern sound. This mixture was to be copied numerous times, even by the firm Gibson itself, which eventually rolled out this electronic guitar in several models. His main Les Paul, which he called "The Grail," was originally cream-colored, but it was decorated with black concentric circles so as to differentiate it from the Les Paul owned by Randy Rhoads, who had also joined Ozzy several years previously. The other Les Paul that Zakk played for a large chunk of his career had even more ink expended on it, for it was adorned with a Confederate flag, the standard of the American South, which symbolizes Southern pride, but also a model for society founded on racism and slavery. Dubbed "The Rebel," this guitar again underwent significant visual alterations when Wylde realized that a member of the glam rock outfit Poison had a Les Paul with similar decorations. Zakk did his utmost to convey the image of a body-building *macho man*, with his long beard and his metal-chain guitar strap, and he had no wish to be associated with these glam rockers, with their make-up and high heels.

He therefore sanded off part of the finish and stuck forty beer-bottle caps to the top, a symbol far more in keeping with his hairy Neanderthal look.

NEXT DOUBLE-PAGE SPREAD
With Ozzy in 1989, during the world tour that followed the release of No Rest For the Wicked, *Ozzy Osbourne's first album featuring Wylde on guitar.*

THE BENCHMARK SOUND

OZZY OSBOURNE
"Miracle Man"
No Rest For the Wicked
(1988)

203

TeleCaSTeR
John 5
TiMe FOR a ReVaMP

John 5 accompanying ▶
the singer Rob Zombie
in 2015 on a Telecaster
produced by the
Custom Shop.

The Deluxe John 5 ▶
Fender Telecaster,
made in Mexico.

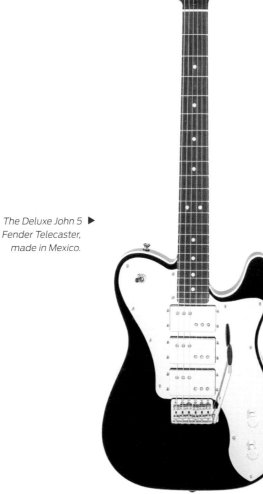

JOHN LOWERY, CHRISTENED JOHN 5 BY
THE SINGER MARILYN MANSON WHEN HE
ACCOMPANIED HIM, LIVED THE LIFE THAT
GUITAR GEEKS the world over dream of: his
professional life was balanced between his role
as sidekick to the singer Rob Zombie, studio
sessions in Los Angeles, and a career as a
virtuoso soloist followed avidly by many lovers
of high-wire guitar acrobatics. John 5 has a
monomaniacal passion for the Telecaster, a
model that he collects with a morbid fervor, and
a somewhat surprising pick given that he is
associated above all with metal, a style in
which the Tele is by no means the obvious
choice. He has a hundred models of it, and at
least one guitar for every year of production
since 1950. The aspect of this character most
likely to stir up jealousy, however, is that he has
worked closely with Fender to design several
models that bear his name.

Over and above John 5's obvious talent,
Fender is also aware of the stakes involved
for a model that bears his name, in that the
firm has to make the Telecaster appealing for
new generations, rather than confining itself
to selling them to nostalgic older customers.
John 5 is the perfect spokesperson for the
younger ones among us. Visually, all his
models play on the contrast between the
black of the body and the chrome of the
pickguard, making it an instantly recognizable
signature model. Add to that his very
personal choice of headstock, which can only
come from a true historian of the company
(in the style of the Telecaster XII, a model
manufactured between 1995 and 1998, for
his two Custom Shops, and in the style of the
Stratocaster from the 1970s for his Mexican
model), and you end up with a new breed of
Teles. As for the sound, John 5 brought
together his career in metal and his
fascination with vintage models by finding
some very elegant compromises: a
humbucker on the bridge and a single-coil
pickup on the neck for the Custom Shop
models, and three vintage-style (Wide
Range) humbuckers for the Mexican model.
Efficient and classy at the same time.

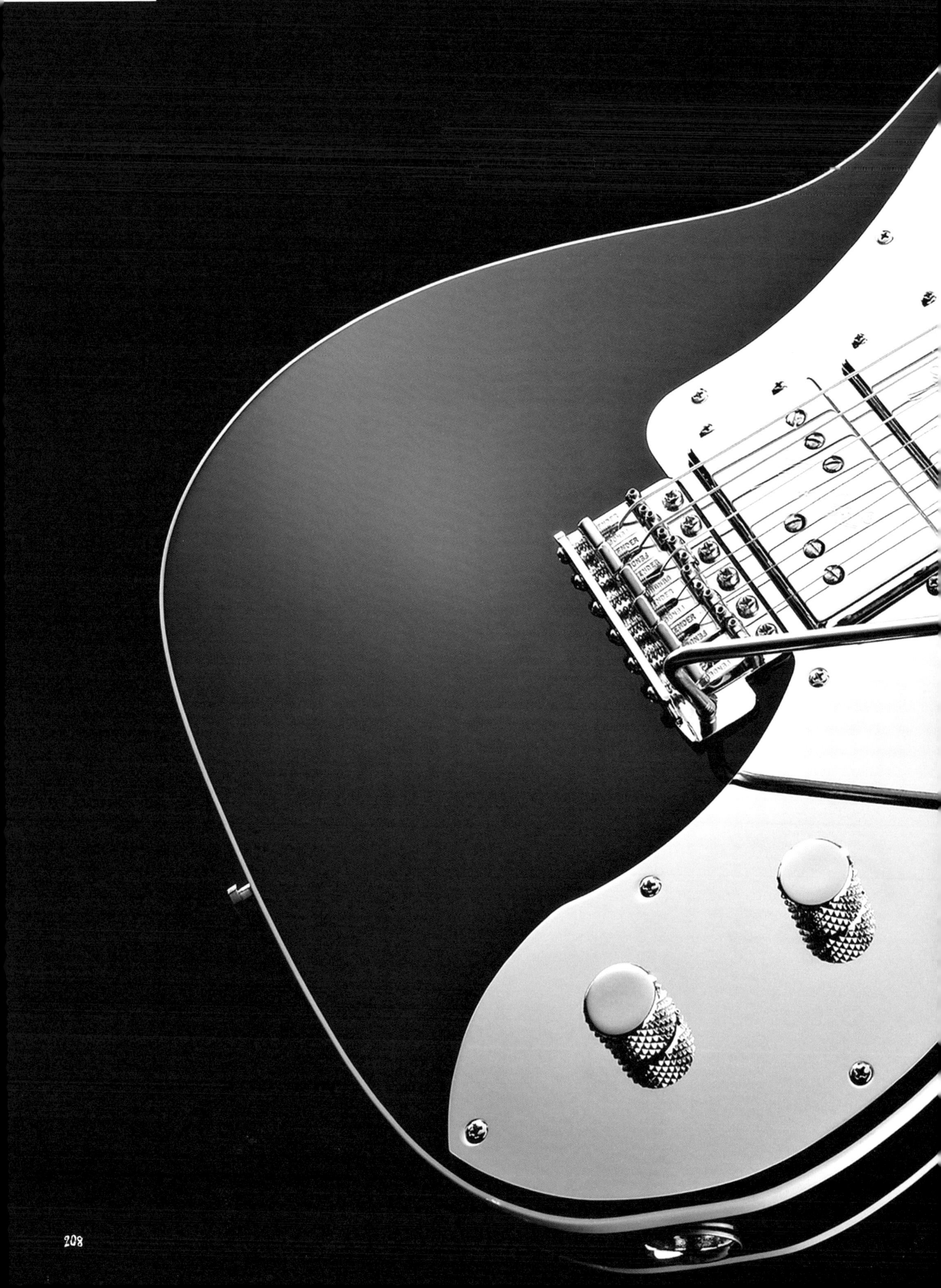

THE BENCHMARK SOUND

JOHN 5 "Sounds Of Impalement"
Requiem (2008)

LES PAUL SIGNATURE BUCKETHEAD

SUPERSIZE ME

EVEN BEFORE YOU HEAR THE BAND'S MUSIC, THE LOOK ADOPTED BY BUCKETHEAD IS ENOUGH TO EVOKE A VERY PARTICULAR UNIVERSE. IN FACT, THIS STRAPPING FELLOW STANDING SIX FOOT FOUR always wears an expressionless white mask inspired by the horror film *Halloween*, and has a KFC bucket on his head (hence the name *Bucket*head) that he uses as a hat and from which his long curly hair hangs down. He was part of the avant-garde jazz-metal band Praxis, and also spent time in Guns N' Roses, but he is best known as a solo artist with a headbanging noise style. With such a distinctive personality, he needed a guitar to match, and he found it in a Les Paul.

Not just any Les Paul, mind you: Buckethead opted for the eternal Gibson, and gave it quite a revamp. He took as his starting point the Les Paul Studio, an affordable model that he cherished due to its lack of extraneous decoration. He asked for the body to be 10% bigger than normal (because he's 10% bigger than the rest of us too!) and, consequently, for the body to be hollowed out, so that it wouldn't be too heavy. The decoration is striking in that this beauty is completely white, from the body to the headstock through the knobs and pickups. Only the fingerboard was left untouched and retains the black hue of the ebony from which it's made. He also chose an extended, 27-inch scale (as opposed to the 24.75-inch scales generally used by Gibson), i.e., a greater string length between the bridge and the nut, for greater tension and thus better resistance in lower tunings. Finally, ceramic pickups with a high level of output are routed through two red kill switches with a look inspired by the buttons on an Atari games console, so that the sound can be killed in an instant. Les Paul himself probably wouldn't have known what to make of this particular Les Paul.

Buckethead in concert, ▶ with a red pick to match the kill switch on his Les Paul.

5 UNLIKELY "MADE IN GIBSON" DESIGNS

FOR ALL THAT GIBSON HAS COME UP WITH SOME DESIGNS THAT MUSICIANS STILL DREAM ABOUT MORE THAN SIXTY YEARS AFTER THEY WERE LAUNCHED, THE MANUFACTURER HAS ALSO CREATED WITH SOME INSTRUMENTS THAT WERE QUIRKY TO SAY THE LEAST. THERE WERE, OF COURSE, THE EXPLORER AND THE FLYING V IN 1958, WHICH WENT OVER LIKE LEAD BALLOONS WHEN THEY FIRST CAME OUT, ONLY FOR POSTERITY TO END UP REHABILITATING THEM TO THE POINT THAT THEY BECAME DESIRABLE. THE FIVE MODELS IN THIS LIST DID NOT HAVE THE SAME DESTINY AND ARE STILL SEEN AS EMBARRASSING HICCUPS IN AN OTHERWISE BEAUTIFUL SAGA.

MARAUDER (1974) ▶

This monstrosity combines the body of a Les Paul Junior with the headstock of a Flying V, an enforced marriage that was never very happy. Designed so as to compete with Fender, it has a bolt-on neck and a single-coil bridge pickup typical of the California-based firm. Despite an endorsement from Paul Stanley of Kiss, who was no doubt keen to pay off his tax bill at the time, the Marauder flopped and is not much sought after even today.

RD (1977) ▶

Eager to keep pace with the trend for synthesizers, Gibson gave its new RD (standing for Research and Development) design active electronics designed by Robert Moog, the godfather of analog synthesis. It was a commendable idea, but guitarists aren't as accepting of new technology as keyboard players, and the series saw only very limited success. Jimmy Page used one on stage, and, more recently, the band Ghost made it their go-to model, in a far more basic electric version.

CORVUS (1982) ▶

The 1980s were a decade in which Gibson struggled, and the manufacturer tried as best it could to keep the public interested, even as the stars of the day swore by their Jackson and Ibanez creations. The Corvus, with its body beveled down and sloping every which way, its bolt-on neck, and its extended headstock, tried to win the public over but only served to convince them that the days when the future of the guitar was decided in Kalamazoo were now far in the past.

MODERNE (1958 OR 1982)

In 1958, when Gibson presented the Explorer and the Flying V to the guitar-playing world, a third patent with an even more radical shape was registered, that of the Moderne. A first re-release came out in 1982 and has since been used by Billy Gibbons, but at present no expert can confirm for certain that the models came off the production line in 1958. A handful of prototypes may perhaps exist, and they are the equivalent of the white whale for the most avid collectors.

FIREBIRD X (2010) ▶

Even today, Gibson continues to indulge in flights of fancy every so often. The Firebird X recreates the shape of the Firebird non-reverse, but with a more flattened and elongated look. Misstep number one, the headstock, with three tuning machines on each side, doesn't work with this shape at all; misstep number two, the maple fingerboard; and finally, misstep number three, the onboard effects that can be controlled by Bluetooth. This effort to reconcile traditional guitar craftsmanship and modern technology was, moreover, retailed at a sky-high price, enough to make sure no one wanted to buy it.

IBANEZ M8M
MESHUGGAH
LOWER AND LOWER

The Ibanez M8M, a model of simplicity.

THE SWEDISH ACT MESHUGGAH IS HELD IN VERY HIGH ESTEEM IN THE WORLD OF METAL FOR HAVING INVENTED THE SUB-GENRE KNOWN AS DJENT, a version of progressive metal that is even lower-pitched and, above all, far and away more complex rhythmically. The guitar parts by Marten Hagstrom and Fredrik Thordendal are like conundrums, in improbable time signatures, all delivered with a sound that seems to have come up from deep within the bowels of the earth.

At the outset, they used Ibanez models with seven strings, then, with the album *Nothing* in 2002, they started tuning them even lower, to such an extent that the luthier Nevborn built two models with eight strings for their next tour! Whereas a seven-string guitar's register goes down to a low *B*, the eighth string brings things right down to an *F* sharp, to really get everyone's insides rumbling, especially given that this string is taken a half step lower, to *F*.

Ibanez, always on the lookout for the next innovation, later suggested that Meshuggah design an eight-string model for them, and the result is uncomplicated but remarkably effective. The M8M is equipped with a solitary ceramic Lundgren humbucker pickup with a very high level of output, and the bridge resembles a Floyd Rose, with its block at the level of the nut, but there is no pin, so it is a way of achieving an attack and a tuning stability similar to those of the Floyd, without the drawbacks. Finally, the scale is 29.4 inches in length as opposed to 25.5 inches on a standard six-string guitar, perfect for keeping the right string tension and preventing the lowest notes from sounding too fuzzy.

The M8M is still Hagstrom's favorite model, but as for Thordendal, he progressed to a model with two, then three humbuckers, with a far more defined shape: the Stoneman, which recreates Ibanez's classic Iceman design with a chrome pickguard. He even kept the logo that the maker used in the 1970s. One foot in the past, but eight strings in the future.

Marten Hagstrom ▶
on stage in 2016.

IBANEZ SIGNATURE
TOSIN ABASI
THE STANDARD BEARER FOR THE NEW GENERATION

The Tosin Abasi signature Ibanez TAM100.

▼

ANIMALS AS LEADERS IS THE FLAGSHIP BAND FOR THE NEW GENERATION IN METAL, WITH AN EXTREMELY CEREBRAL INSTRUMENTAL APPROACH. The trio is led by Tosin Abasi, a man who single-handedly represents the tastes and aspirations of all guitarists when they are new at the instrument: he plays on an eight-string Ibanez influenced by Meshuggah, experiments with multiple scales, and only plays on virtual amps.

Ibanez, first of all: Abasi developed two signature eight-string models in collaboration with the manufacturer: the TAM10 and the TAM100, the latter being the more visually impressive of the two. It features the traditional RG shape with a maple top for a more precise attack, perfect as it doesn't have an ill-defined eighth string, and a pickup configuration that offers an abundance of possibilities (two humbuckers and a single-

coil controlled by a five-way switch and two splits), vital for dealing with the rich and diverse textures of the band's music. Next up was multiscale: on his prototype Ibanez with its crazy shape, the bass strings stretch further down the neck, hence the fanned frets. The aim is to have more tension in the bass strings, while preserving the sensations derived from standard playing in the treble strings.

And lastly, virtual amps: nowadays, simulators like the Fractal Axe FX are a great way of creating an amp without having to get out of the machine, staying 100% digital. Modernity in the guitar world has a face, and it's Tosin Abasi's.

JACKSON JUGGERNAUT
MISHA MANSOOR
THE SUPERSTRAT REINVENTS ITSELF

FOR NUMEROUS BANDS IN THE NEW GENERATION, THE OLD GUITARS NO LONGER HAD THE SAME APPEAL: they were far more interested in what the instrument could do for them, and did not overly concern themselves with age, rarity, or value. In this, we see the impulse of the hot rod assemblers from the 1980s, who took the parts they liked and turned them into their perfect model.

Misha Mansoor, the leader of the djent band Periphery, went through multiple modern brands during the course of his brief career: Strandberg, Aristides, Mayones, Skervesen, Daemoness...In the end, he put his name to a signature model with Jackson, one of the oldest makers on whose guitars he played, and that lived up to his expectations. His Juggernaut model was the Superstrat of the year 2017. On a shape akin to that of the Dinky (Jackson's radical Strat), Mansoor added a maple top (for greater precision and for visual appeal), a fixed bridge, and two Bare Knuckle Juggernaut pickups, designed for Mansoor and combining the pugnacity of the ceramic magnet with the roundness of the alnico. Very close to being just what the artist needed to make his vision a reality.

THE BENCHMARK SOUND

PERIPHERY
"Marigold"
Select Difficulty (2016)

▲
A superb blue version of the Jackson Juggernaut.

217

MUSICMAN SIGNATURE
ST. VINCENT
UNEXPLORED TERRITORY

Annie Clark during a promotional photo-shoot to present the new colors of her Music Man model, early in 2017. ▶

ST. VINCENT IS THE STAGE NAME OF THE GUITARIST AND SINGER ANNIE CLARK, THE ICONOCLAST OF INDIE ROCK WHO IS GRADUALLY COMING TO THE FORE as the archetypal modern guitarist, her relationship to the instrument as adventurous as it is loving. The guitar she played in the early days was a Harmony Bobkat, a cheap monstrosity from the 1960s, whose garage rock and anti-establishment esthetic suited her down to the ground. In the end, though, it was the signature Albert Lee model (Lee was a British country guitarist) produced by Music Man that won her heart. Music Man is the second firm set up by Leo Fender after he was released from the contractual obligations which tied him to the maker that bears his name, and its range of instruments, made in California, principally consists of models designed by seasoned guitarists such as Steve Lukather (Toto), Steve Morse (Deep Purple), and John Petrucci (Dream Theater). The marriage was finally consecrated early in 2016, when St. Vincent became the first female artist to be given a signature model by Music Man. And she didn't confine herself to a mere variation on a familiar theme — far from it. The shape is unprecedented, at once refined and perfectly ergonomic. It's possible to see in it a distant connection to the Firebird non-reverse, an oddity dreamed up by Gibson dating from the late 1960s, but the St. Vincent is far more elegant. As for the pickup configuration, that too is rarely explored territory, with three humbuckers for a hybrid

sound that's somewhere between a more solid Strat and a snappier Les Paul. The picture is completed by the vibrato arm made by Music Man itself, and even the finish is as personal as it gets, for Annie designed the particular shade of blue that adorns her model herself.

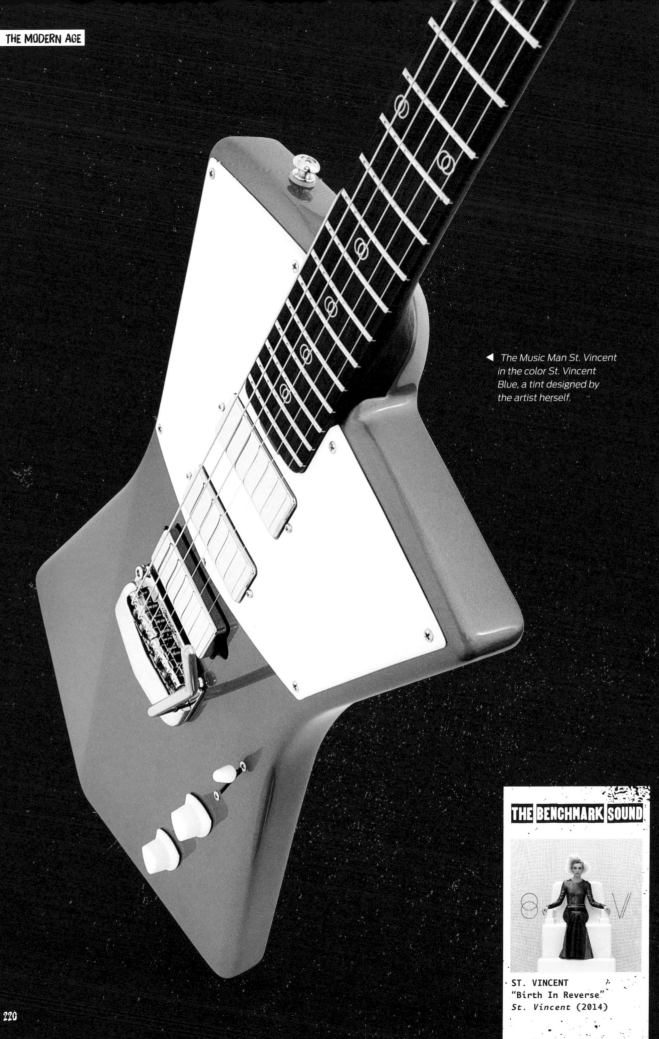

◀ The Music Man St. Vincent in the color St. Vincent Blue, a tint designed by the artist herself.

THE BENCHMARK SOUND

ST. VINCENT
"Birth In Reverse"
St. Vincent (2014)

manson
MATTHEW BELLAMY
EFFECTS On BOaRD

AS THE LEADER OF THE MOST POPULAR ROCK TRIO OF THE 21ST CENTURY, MATTHEW BELLAMY HAS DEVELOPED AN AVANT-GARDE approach both in his method of songwriting and, especially, in his choice of sounds. By contrast with Coldplay or even Radiohead, who took what The Edge had done and ran with it by using effects as the basis of their textures, Bellamy has rehabilitated the majesty of the riff and the guitar solo, bringing together effects as a chef might sprinkle spices over a dish that already has a wonderfully strong flavor.

The guitar he loves most was created by the British luthier Hugh Manson. Its shape has a little of the Telecaster about it, but any resemblance to its venerable ancestor ends there. The MB-1 (for that is its name) has seen several different pickup configurations depending on Bellamy's needs and wants, but generally with a humbucker on the bridge and a single-coil pickup (often a P90) in the neck position, the two both routed through a kill switch, for sharp and abrupt sound-killing effects. What makes Matthew's Mansons really interesting, though, is their incorporation of effect pedal circuits. It's not a new idea, and Bo Diddley was among the first to try to put something like that together, but in Bellamy's case, this added touch is executed to perfection. There are two effects that he favors: the Phase 90 by MXR and above all the Fuzz Factory by Zvex, a far richer and louder upgrade of the Fuzz Face, which became the manufacturer of choice for his band Muse.

The most fascinating instrument of the lot, though, is without question the Korg Kaoss Pad, a control panel for effects built into some of his guitars. It enables him to control the fuzz in real time and thereby obtain cries, groans, hooting noises, and other strange, but very satisfying, sounds. What's more, it was such a good idea that Ibanez turned it into a whole new model, the RGKP6.

THE BENCHMARK SOUND

MUSE ORIGIN OF SYMMETRY

MUSE "Plug In Baby"
Origin Of Symmetry
(2001)

Matthew Bellamy ▶
on stage with Muse in 2009.

◄ Josh Homme
in 2013 armed with his
MotorAve BelAire.

▲
The Maton BB1200 JH,
the singer's Australian
signature model.

Maton JOSH HOMME

THE NEW HERO

MODERN-DAY GUITAR-MAKING HAS ATTAINED A LEVEL OF QUALITY THAT WASN'T EASY TO COME BY JUST ONE OR TWO DECADES AGO. The big brands are no longer the safe investment they once were, and hundreds of smaller, very talented craftspeople are coming up with very effective solutions, as much as everyone remains conscious of the sheer weight of history that the behemoths of the industry represent. In spite of that, rock is still very much under the sway of these big names, such is the extent to which the guitar heroes who people the genre have not yet been emancipated from the mythology of the greats of yesteryear. Josh Homme has found his own voice and, while he is clearly inspired by Led Zeppelin and also Black Sabbath, he doesn't try to reproduce the sounds of Page or Iommi; on the contrary, he has spent years honing a texture that is entirely his own. He even jealously keeps the maker of his studio amps and pedals a secret.

As for the guitars, it's hard to be quite so discreet, and in this field, Josh Homme has been careful always to steer clear of the beaten track. When he played for the band Kyuss, he tended to play a solid-body Ovation, a brand, however, that's known for its electro-acoustic guitars and whose efforts on the electric side have never enjoyed much success. In Queens of the Stone Age, he was seen with a Telecaster and Ephiphone Dots (copies of the very affordable ES-335), but two models keep on coming back. The Maton

BB1200, which even became his signature model, is an archtop ES-335-style guitar made in Australia by a firm known above all for its acoustic guitars, and the MotorAve BelAire is another creation derived from the ES-335 manufactured in a small workshop in North Carolina. Consistent, but never predictable.

QUEENS OF THE STONE AGE
"Little Sister"
Lullabies To Paralyze
(2005)

5 ALBUMS FEATURING UNUSUAL GUITAR SOUNDS

MOST GUITARISTS, HAVING GROWN UP LISTENING TO THE SAME INFLUENCES, END UP HAVING FAIRLY SIMILAR SOUNDS, ALL THE MORE SO GIVEN THAT, ULTIMATELY, THERE AREN'T MANY OF THE GREAT GUITAR MODELS AND THE FINEST AMPS. FOR ALL THAT, GREAT MUSICIANS DISTINGUISH THEMSELVES BY FINDING A WAY TO CREATE A RECOGNIZABLE TEXTURE FROM THE VERY FIRST NOTE, AND SOME OF THE MOST ADVENTUROUS OF THEM HAVEN'T HELD BACK FROM PUTTING THEIR SOUND THROUGH TORTURE, USING A WIDE RANGE OF EFFECTS IN ORDER TO ATTAIN UNPRECEDENTED SONIC PHENOMENA.

KING CRIMSON, ▶ DISCIPLINE (1981) TRACK: "ELEPHANT TALK"

Robert Fripp has always sought a very personal sound in King Crimson, but on this album, it is the second guitarist, Adrian Belew, who takes the honors, by managing to evoke an elephant's trumpeting with his Strat and a few pedals. The transition in the song is so bizarre that it makes you feel uneasy.

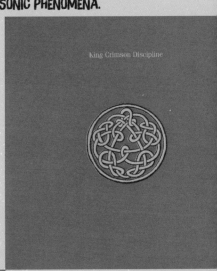

King Crimson Discipline

THE SMITHS, ▶ HATFUL OF HOLLOW (1984) TRACK: "HOW SOON IS NOW?"

The sound of Johnny Marr, guitarist of The Smiths, is often drowned out in the chorus, but on "How Soon Is Now?," he was seeking a well-defined beat. He therefore turned to a tremolo, but in order to get a deeper, polyrhythmic effect, he used five at the same time, on the same number of Fender Twin amps. The result is mind-blowing.

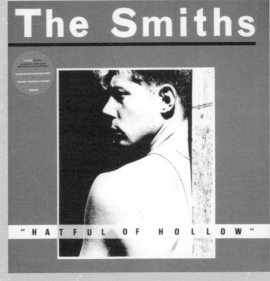

**STEVE VAI, ►
PASSION AND WARFARE (1990)
TRACK: "EROTIC NIGHTMARES"**

This album is the one that brought Vai
to the attention of the whole world,
and several songs on it are composed
entirely of bizarre noises generated by the
multi-effect Eventide H3000, which is
straightforwardly credited as an instrument
in its own right. The transition in "Erotic
Nightmares," though, with its strange, flute-
like sound, is the one that wins the award
for the dreamiest, most fantastical music.

**◄ DAVID BOWIE,
EARTHLING (1997)
TRACK: "LITTLE WONDER"**

Bowie always displayed considerable talent
in his choice of collaborators, and, when he
decided to delve into electronic music in the
mid-1990s, he did so with one of the most
inventive guitarists of the time, Reeves Gabrels.
Gabrels pulls violently at his vibrato arm, makes
the springs vibrate, and extracts a sound from
his Parker that is as acidic as it is brash.

**RAGE AGAINST ►
THE MACHINE,
THE BATTLE OF LOS
ANGELES (1999)
TRACK: "ASHES IN THE FALL"**

Tom Morello was among the most
inventive and cutting-edge guitarists
of the 1990s. Even though the
broader public discovered him in
1992 with the first album by Rage
Against the Machine, it is in The
Battle of Los Angeles that he is at his
pinnacle, as in the intro to "Ashes In
the Fall," where he makes his guitar
sound like a broken video game.

Joe Bonamassa

WELCOME TO NERDVILLE

THE NEW STAR OF BLUES ROCK JOE BONAMASSA IS A GUITAR-LOVER OF A VERY SPECIFIC KIND: HE'S A COLLECTOR.
Most musicians who have amassed a large collection, like Billy Gibbons or Joe Perry (Aerosmith), have done so over a the course of a career spanning many years, by buying old guitars at a time when no one was using the term "vintage." Bonamassa is the son of the owner of a specialist store, and so he was brought up well aware of what genuine collector's items looked like. He has always invested a large portion of the money he had at his disposal in vintage instruments, collector's amps, and even old promotional material, *memorabilia* in all its forms. He even has a special name for the expeditions that he undertakes, in search of rare pearls in guitar shops all over the world, during his tours: they're Guitar Safaris. This obsession generally triggers two kinds of reaction: some fans admire the fact that a professional musician takes these priceless guitars on tour and lets them live rather than leaving them shut away in a safe, but the more jealous types criticize his spoiled-child approach in amassing these gorgeous instruments like so many toys that are cast aside as soon as their novelty wears off.

The photos and video footage of the house in which he keeps his flock are very impressive, and he himself refers to them as his Nerdville museum, taking full ownership of his status as a vintage guitar nerd. Among his best-loved items, it's clear he has a strong affection for Bursts, the Les Paul Standards from 1958, 1959, or 1960, which he has done a great deal to bring back in fashion, and which he has confirmed as the Holy Grail for all dedicated collectors. Each of the eight Bursts in his collection has its own nickname and backstory, and some of them have been cloned by the Gibson Custom Shop as part of limited editions in the Collector's Choice series. The "Principal Skinner" 59 has long been his favorite, and inherited this nickname as a nod to the Simpsons character, because it was purchased at auction from Skinner Auctioneers. "The Babe" is a 1960 model with a Bigsby vibrato arm with unusual little wings, hence its other nickname, "Batman." The rarest of them all is the Blackburst, a 1960 model repainted in black before it left the factory at the request of a customer who couldn't afford to buy a Custom but wanted a black guitar all the same. His fallback option was the Standard, and so he unwittingly created a fascinating historical anomaly.

NEXT DOUBLE-PAGE SPREAD
Bonamassa on stage in 2015 accompanied by his creation, the Bonabyrd.

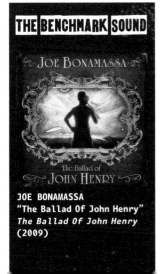

JOE BONAMASSA
"The Ballad Of John Henry"
The Ballad Of John Henry
(2009)

A KID IN A CANDY STORE

Not content to collaborate with Gibson with a view to making replicas of his rare pieces, Joe Bonamassa also designed several signature models, which are not necessarily copies of beauties from times gone by. His most remarkable creation is the Bonabyrd, a hybrid with the body of a Les Paul and the headstock of a Firebird, in a superb Pelham Blue color. This is also the tint chosen for his Epiphone Les Paul Standard Outfit, an attempt to offer a good, vintage-style Les Paul at a reduced price. There is even a variation of this model in Inverness Green with a Bigsby, an amalgamation of various old models that had never been put together. Through these different models, Bonamassa was living the dream of countless guitar fans who long to design their own Gibson from scratch and see it rolled out as a new model.

◀ *The Gibson Joe Bonamassa Bonabyrd, a model designed by the guitarist in 2015.*

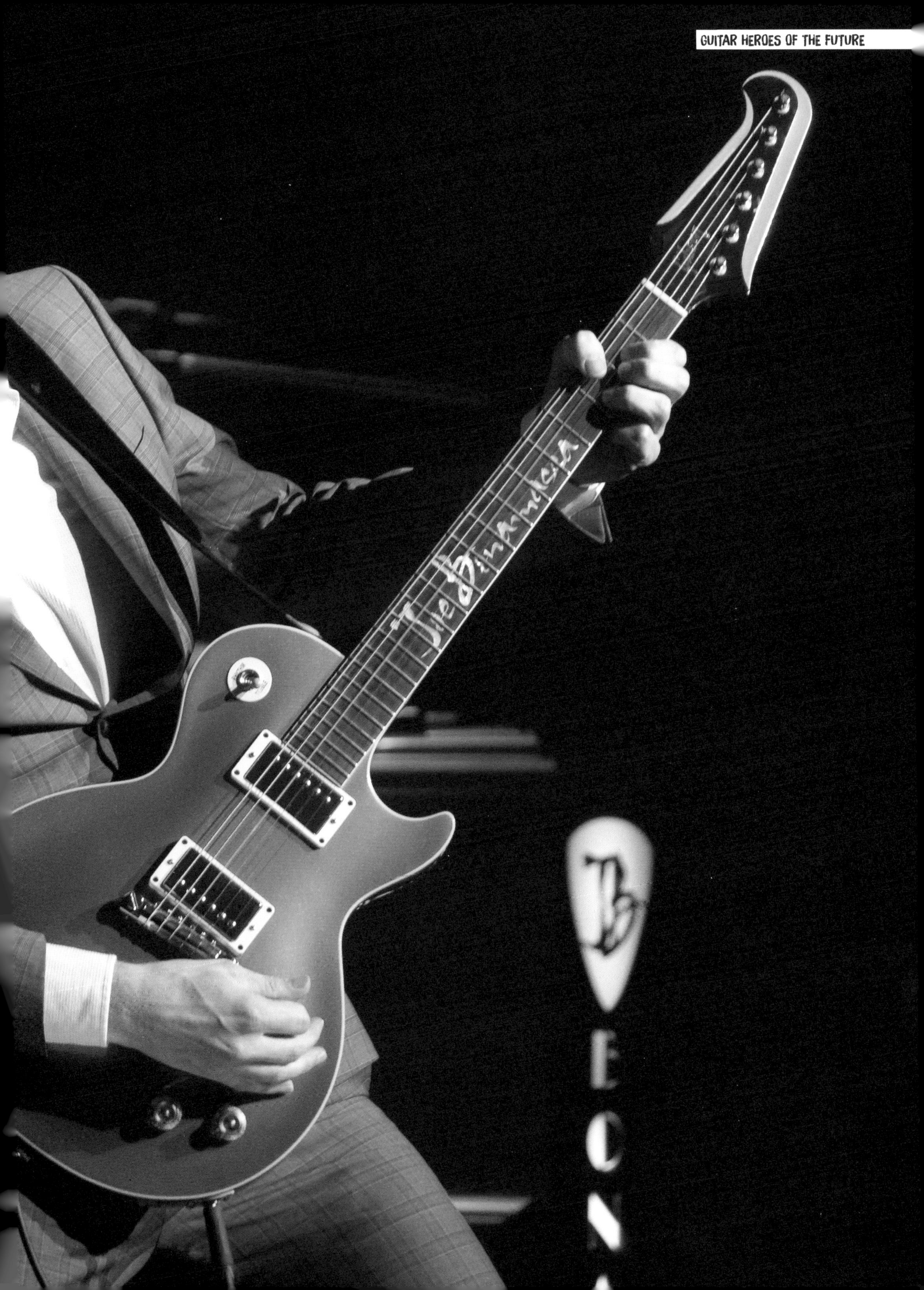

DOUBLeBFOOT
RON THAL
THe EXTRA-TERRESTRIAL

◄ *Ron Thal and the second version of his Vigier DoubleBfoot.*

HiS NAME MAY NOT BE THE MOST WELL-KNOWN iN THE GUITAR FiRMAMENT, BUT HE'S NONETHELESS ONE OF THE MOST iNNOVATiVE, gifted, and fascinating musicians active today. Ron Thal, aka Bumblefoot, started out as a shredder in the late 1980s, and even then was trying to break out of this overly restrictive format by introducing the sense of humor that could be seen even in his guitars, from the famous Swiss Cheese Grater (the emmental guitar, an Ibanez painted yellow and pockmarked with holes) to the Foot Guitar, a foot-shaped Vigier with black and yellow stripes and two wings that come out of each side of the body when the vibrato arm is activated.

He joined Guns N' Roses in 2006, replacing Buckethead, and regularly switches between a Les Paul, the indispensable guitar at the heart of the band that will forever retain the marks of Slash's influence, and a fretless Vigier. Patrice Vigier is a French luthier who set up his own firm in 1980, and who has since helped further research into the instrument through numerous innovations. Among them, he has perfected the concept of the fretless guitar, an idea borrowed from the violin and double bass, but one that nobody has adopted as much as Ron Thal. As a result of switching from one guitar to another, he ended up wanting to put them both together in a single guitar with two necks, the DoubleBfoot. This 13-pound monster combines a fretless neck and a fretted neck for a very unusual result, with a

shape that is angular without being aggressive. There are three versions: one with a gold finish, another with a matt black finish, and a version with psychedelic painting that takes the notion of a unique instrument into new territory. It isn't for everyone — and that's exactly the point.

BUMBLEFOOT
"R2"
Uncool (2000)

233

SIGNATURE CHARVEL
GUTHRIE GOVAN
THE ARISTOCRAT

GUTHRIE GOVAN REPRESENTS THE OLD GUARD OF THE SHRED FUSION OF THE 1980S, WHO MANAGED TO FIND FRESH INSPIRATION AND ADAPT TO CHANGING MUSICAL FASHIONS.

He is now known as the guitarist for the progressive genius of Steven Wilson, as a performer for the film score composer Hans Zimmer, and as the leader of the instrumental trio The Aristocrats, a collective whose success has been as dazzling as improbable. Having spent a while as an ambassador for guitars by Suhr, an American maker very fond of the Superstrat, he now has a signature model with Charvel.

The Charvel Guthrie Govan Signature brings together all the enhancements made to the Strat since the 1980s: the twenty-four-fret neck has a compound radius for a faster playing feel on the treble strings, the jumbo frets are made of stainless steel, the original Floyd Rose vibrato arm was chosen due to the denser sound it makes, the locking tuners enable better maintenance of the tuning, the pickups are two humbuckers and a single-coil designed by Charvel and controlled using a five-position switch, and finally the basswood body is covered with a superb flame maple top whose beauty is brought out by the natural finish. This guitar is a whole toolset in itself, one capable of dealing with all the textures that its various uses require. With a single flick of the switch, the guitarist can move from a bright, Stratoid sound to an ample, Gibsonesque degree of saturation, all

Guthrie Govan on stage ▶ in 2015 in Steven Wilson's band.

on a Charvel that feels so good to play that its owner forgets it's even there in his or her hands. And that is in fact precisely what some say is the problem with this kind of guitar — that they make guitarists forget they're there, without leading guitarists in any particular direction. Govan himself has shown signs of wanting to find a more marked personality, as, for in two tracks on the album *Tres Caballeros*, he used a Gretsch 6120 for the recording, one of the most capricious and unruly guitars out there, yet so inspiring.

▲
Jack White in 2005 at a White Stripes concert in Glasgow.

THE BENCHMARK SOUND

THE WHITE STRIPES
"Black Math"
Elephant (2003)

AIRLINE JACK WHITE

BACK TO THE FUTURE

JACK WHITE IS THE POLAR OPPOSITE OF THE SCHOOL OF GUITARISTS WHO GO SEEKING A WELL-HONED TOOL THAT WILL PERFECTLY FULFILL THEIR EVERY WISH.
As rightful heir of the bluesmen of the Delta such as Son House or Charley Patton, White seeks an instrument with a hardened personality, a piece of wood that gives him a challenge and doesn't follow his orders to the letter. The battle against the guitar is an essential element of his playing style, particularly in the White Stripes, where this tension was like the third member of an explosive duo.

On his own, he brought the cheap guitars from the 1950s and 1960s back into fashion. At the time, the major guitar manufacturers were creating their masterpieces, but less-fortunate guitarists had to make do with more roughly-made equipment that generally came from the Valco, Harmony, or Kay factories.

The guitars made by these three giants were given brand names that varied depending on where they were going to be sold. Valco made guitars for, among others, the retail chain Montgomery Ward, so this is the name that adorns White's beloved guitar. Better known under the brand name Airline, this guitar model was originally the signature instrument of the bluesman from Chicago J.B. Hutto. Its quirky shape and red and white colors made it ideal for the color scheme adopted by the White Stripes, and its grungy sound made it appropriate for their garage rock. Add to that a hollow fiberglass body that easily picks up feedback, another crucial component of Jack White's sound, and you get a guitar that's the perfect choice because of its very flaws. Following this prestigious use of the instrument, the Airlines from the 1960s became unaffordable, but those who tried to copy them by grabbing a J.B. Hutto in hopes of finding White's sound have missed the point: you've got to find a guitar whose imperfections are what you love most about it.

INDEX

Page numbers in italics represent photos

CREDITS

Cover, top : © Monitor Picture Library/Photoshot/Getty Images ; bottom : © Nigel Osbourne/Redferns/Getty Images ; back cover: © Gibson. p. 6 top : © Michael Ochs Archives/Getty Images ; bottom : © deepspacedave/Shutterstock.com ; p. 8 vignette : D.R. ; right : Domaine public ; p. 9 : © Gibson ; p. 10 : © Bernard Hoffman - Time Life Contributer/Getty Images ; p. 11 : Library of Congress, Washington, D.C. ; p. 12 : D.R./domaine public ; p. 13 top et bottom : © C.F. Martin Archives ; p. 14 : © C.F. Martin Archives ; p. 15 : D.R. ; p. 16-17 : D.R. ; p. 18 : © Gibson ; p. 19 : © Al Aumuller/Library of Congress, Washington, D.C. ; p. 20 left : © C.F. Martin Archives ; right : Domaine public ; p. 21 top left : © C.F. Martin Archives ; center right : D.R. ; vignette : D.R. ; p. 22 vignette : D.R. ; right : © Josh Withers/Shutterstock.com ; p. 23 : © C.F. Martin Archives ; p. 24 : © C.F. Martin Archives ; vignette : D.R. ; p. 25 top : © Nito/Shutterstock.com ; bottom : © OlD.R.ich/Shutterstock. com ; p. 26 : Domaine Public ; p. 27 vignette : © Getty Images ; center : © Michael J. Malone ; p. 28 : © Fender ; p. 29 : © Michael Ochs Archives/Getty Images ; p. 30 : © Gibson ; p. 31 : © Michael Ochs Archives/Getty Images ; p. 32 vignette : D.R. ; right : Gretsch Guitar News/Domaine public ; p. 33 : © Fender ; p. 34 : © Michael Ochs Archives/Getty Images ; vignette : D.R. ; p. 35 : © Fender ; p. 36 : © Keystone/Getty Images ; p. 37 vignette : D.R. ; p. 38-39 : D.R. ; p. 40 : © Gibson ; p. 41 : © collection Henry Ruggeri ; p. 42 left : © Gretsch Guitar News ; p. 43 : © Paul Natkin/Getty Images ; p. 44 : © Michael Ochs Archives/Getty Images ; p. 45 : © Gibson ; vignette : D.R. ; p. 46 vignette : D.R. ; p. 46-47 : © David Redfern/Redferns/Getty Images ; p. 48 vignette : D.R. ; p. 49 : © ITV/REX/Shutterstock ; p. 50-51 : D.R. ; p. 52 vignette : D.R. ; right : © JP Jazz Archive/Redferns/GettyImages ; p. 53 left : © Gibson ; vignette : D.R. ; p. 54 : © Popperfoto/Getty Images ; p. 55 : © Gibson ; p. 56-57 : © David Redfern/Redferns ; p. 57 vignette : D.R. ; p. 58 : © William Gottlieb/Redferns/GettyImages ; vignette : D.R. ; p. 59 : © JP Jazz Archive/Redferns/Getty Images ; p. 60 : © Gibson ; p. 61 © David Redfern/Redferns/GettyImages ; p. 62 left : D.R. ; right : © Gibson ; p. 63 (pleine page) : © Gibson ; bottom droit : © Sergey Goryachev/Shutterstock.com, Sergey Goryachev/Shutterstock.com, Olga Popova/Shutterstock.com ; p. 64-65 : © David Redfern/Redferns/Getty Images ; p. 65 bottom : D.R. ; p. 66 : © Gibson ; p. 67 : © Paul Natkin/WireImage/Getty Images ; p. 68-69 : © Terry O'Neill/Getty Images ; p. 69 vignette : D.R. ; p. 70 : © Gibson ; p. 71 : © GAB Archive/Redferns/Getty Images ; p. 72-73 : © Gibson ; p. 74 : © Gibson ; p. 75 : © Graham Wiltshire/Redferns/Getty Images ; p. 76-77 : © Waring Abbott/Getty Images ; p. 78 : © Fender ; p. 79 : © Terry O'Neill/Getty Images ; p. 80-81 : © C.F. Martin Archives ; p. 82 left : © Dick Barnatt/Redferns/Getty Images ; right : © Gibson ; p. 83 : © Estate of Keith Morris/Redferns/Getty Images ; p. 84 top : © Fred Duval/FilmMagic/Getty Images ; bottom : Gibson ; p. 86 : © Fender ; p. 87 : © Michael Ochs Archives/Getty Images ; vignette : D.R. ; p. 88 left : D.R. ; right : Domaine public ; p. 89 : © Hulton-Deutsch Collection/Corbis via Getty Images ; vignette : D.R. ; p. 90 vignette : D.R. ; bottom droit : © Michael Ochs Archives/Getty Images ; p. 91 : © Gibson ; p. 93 : © Bentley Archive/Popperfoto/Getty Images ; p. 94 : © Ed Caraeff/Getty Images ; vignette : D.R. ; p. 95 : © John D Kisch/Separate Cinema Archive/Getty Images ; p. 96 left et right : © Gibson ; vignette : D.R. ; p. 97 : © Gai Terrell/Redferns/Getty Images ; p. 98 : © Michael Putland/Getty Images ; p. 99 left : D.R. ; vignette : D.R. ; p. 100 : © David Lefranc/Gamma-Rapho via Getty Images ; p. 101 left : D.R. ; vignette : D.R. ; p. 102 : © Fender ; p. 103 : © Fender ; vignette : D.R. ; p. 104-105 : © Erica Echenberg/Redferns/Getty Images ; p. 106 top : D.R. ; bottom left : D.R. ; bottom droit : D.R. ; p. 107 top : © Julien Bitoun ; bottom : © Joby Sessions/Guitarist Magazine via Getty Images ; p. 108 vignette : D.R. ; p. 109 : © David Redfern/Redferns/Getty Images ; p. 110 : © Michael Ochs Archives/Getty Images ; p. 111 : © Gibson ; p. 112 © Lindsay Brice/Getty Images ; p. 113 : © Donna Santisi/Redferns/Getty Images ; p. 114 : © Gibson ; p. 115 left and right : © Fender ; p. 116 vignette : D.R., p. 117 : © Dick Barnatt/Redferns/Getty Images ; p. 118-119 : © Michael Putland/Getty Images ; p. 120 : © Michael Ochs Archives/Getty Images ; p. 121 : © Fender ; p. 122 vignette : D.R. ; p. 123 : © Rob Verhorst/Redferns/Getty Images ; p. 124-125 : © George Rose/Getty Images ; p. 126-127 : D.R. ; p. 128 : © Gibson ; p. 129 : © David Corio/Redferns/Getty Images ; p. 130 : © Michael Putland/Getty Images ; p. 131 left : © Gibson ; vignette : D.R. ; p. 132 : © Ian Dickson/Redferns/Getty Images ; p. 133 : D.R. ; p. 134 vignette : D.R. ; p. 134-135 : © Michael Ochs Archives/Getty Images ; p. 136 vignette : D.R. ; right : © Stephen J. Boitano/LightRocket via Getty Images ; p. 137 vignette : D.R. ; left : © Gibson ; right : © Lynn Goldsmith/Corbis/VCG via Getty Images ; p. 138 : © Paul Natkin/WireImage ; p. 139 vignette : D.R. ; p. 140 vignette : D.R. ; p. 141 : © Waring Abbott/Getty Images ; p. 142-143 : © Waring Abbott/Getty Images ; p. 144 left : D.R. ; vignette : D.R. ; p. 145 : © Clayton Call/Redferns/Getty Images ; p. 146 : © Fender ; p. 147 left : © Fender ; vignette : D.R. ; right : © Nikola Spasenoski/Shutterstock.com ; p. 148 : © Fender ; p. 149 : © Peter Still/Redferns/GettyImages ; vignette : D.R. ; p. 150 : © Knips/Dalle ; p. 151 top et bottom left : © Rick Turner ; vignette : D.R. ; p. 152 top : D.R. ; bottom : Shutterstock.com ; p. 153 top : D.R. ; center : Digitech ; bottom : D.R. ; p. 154-155 : © Gibson ; p. 157 : © Gibson ; p. 158 vignette : D.R. ; p. 158-159 : © Larry Marano/Getty Images ; p. 160 vignette : D.R. ; top : © Fender ; p. 161 : © Steve Thorne/Redferns/Getty Images ; p. 162 : © Gibson ; p. 163 : © Ebet Roberts/Redferns/Getty Images ; p. 164 : © Peter Still/Redferns/GettyImages ; p. 165 : © Richard E. Aaron/Redferns/Getty Images ; p. 166 : © Fender ; p. 167 : © setzerarchive.com ; p. 168 vignette : D.R. ; p. 169 : © Brian Rasic/Getty Images ; p. 170 top et bottom : © HTD ; p. 172 top : © Fender ; vignette : D.R. ; p. 173 : © Kevin Mazur/WireImage/Getty Images ; p. 174 : © Gary Wolstenholme/Redferns via Getty Images ; p. 176 : © Tony Woolliscroft/WireImage/Getty Images ; p. 177 : © Martin Philbey/Redferns/Getty Images ; p. 178 : © Fender ; p. 179 left : © Fender ; right top : © Christian Bertrand/Shutterstock.com ; right bottom : © Christian Bertrand/Shutterstock.com ; p. 180 left : © Fender ; bottom : © Fender ; right : D.R. ; p. 181 : © Fender ; p. 182 left : D.R. ; right : © Fender ; p. 183 top : © Fender ; bottom : © Ibanez ; right : © Gibson ; p. 184 : © Scott Dudelson/WireImage/Getty Images ; p. 186 vignette : D.R. ; p. 187 : © Michael Hurcomb/Corbis via Getty Images ; p. 188-189 : © Ross Halfin.com/Dalle ; p. 189 vignette : D.R. ; p. 191 : © Sterling Munksgard/Shutterstock.com ; p. 193 : © Rob Sanahan/Dalle ; p. 194 : © Tim Mosenfelder/ImageDirect/Getty Images ; p. 195 : D.R. ; p. 197 : © Jordi Vidal/Redferns ; p. 198-199 : © Frans Schellekens/Redferns ; p. 199 vignette : D.R. ; p. 201 : © David Tan/Shinko Music/Getty Images ; p. 202 : © Jim Steinfeldt/Michael Ochs Archives/Getty Images ; p. 203 vignette : D.R. ; p. 204-205 : © Paul Natkin/WireImage/Getty Images ; p. 206 : © Fender ; p. 207 : © Raymond Boyd/Getty Images ; p. 208-209 : © Fender ; p. 209 vignette : D.R. ; p. 211 : © C. Flanigan/WireImage/Getty Images ; p. 212-213 : © Gibson ; p. 214 : © Ibanez ; p. 215 : © Francesco Prandoni/Redferns/Getty Images ; p. 216 : D.R. ; p. 217 vignette : D.R. ; center : Fender ; p. 218, 219, 220 : © Music Man ; p. 220 vignette : D.R. ; p. 221 : © Music Man ; p. 222 vignette : D.R. ; p. 223 © Richard Lautens/Toronto Star/Getty Images ; p. 224 top : © yakub88/Shutterstock.com ; center : © Maton ; p. 225 vignette : D.R. ; p. 226-227 : D.R. ; p. 228 vignette : D.R. ; p. 229 : © Gibson ; p. 230-231 : © Matthew Baker/WireImage/Getty Images ; p. 232 : © Catherine Asanov ; p. 233 vignette : D.R. ; p. 234 : © Roberto Ricciuti/Redferns via Getty Images ; p. 235 : © Fender ; p. 236 : © Ross Gilmore/Redferns/GettyImages ; vignette : D.R.

Although we have made every effort to secure correct permssions for the images used in this book, the publishers invite the owners of these images to advise us of any changes that may be required for future printings, and thanks them in advance.